WHOLENESS

WINNING IN LIFE FROM THE INSIDE OUT

TOURÉ ROBERTS

ZONDERVAN®

ZONDERVAN

Wholeness
Copyright © 2018 by Touré Roberts

Requests for information should be addressed to:
Zondervan, *3900 Sparks Dr. SE, Grand Rapids, Michigan 49546*

Zondervan titles may be purchased in bulk for educational, business, fundraising, or promotional use. For information, please email SpecialMarkets@Zondervan.com.

ISBN 978-0-310-35938-8 (softcover)

ISBN 978-0-310-35394-2 (special edition)

ISBN 978-0-310-35319-5 (audio)

ISBN 978-0-310-35253-2 (ebook)

Library of Congress Cataloging-in-Publication Data

Names: Roberts, Touré, author.
Title: Wholeness : winning in life from the inside out / Touré Roberts.
Description: Grand Rapids, Michigan : Zondervan, [2018]
Identifiers: LCCN 2017044656 | ISBN 9780310351948 (hardcover)
Subjects: LCSH: Excellence--Religious aspects--Christianity. | Christian life. |
    Identity (Psychology)--Religious aspects--Christianity.
Classification: LCC BV4509.5 .R624 2018 | DDC 248.4--dc23 LC record available at
    https://lccn.loc.gov/2017044656

The author is represented by Dupree Miller and Associates.

Cover design: Jennifer McMillan
Cover photography: Dana Patrick
Interior design: Kait Lamphere

Printed in the United States of America

19 20 21 22 23 24 25 26 27 28 29 /LSC/ 15 14 13 12 11 10 9 8 7 6 5 4 3 2 1

I dedicate this book to all of God's creation from every tribe, language, nation, and culture. Humanity, this one's for you.

CONTENTS

FOREWORD BY T. D. JAKES

One doesn't have to live a long time before realizing that neither the multi-billion-dollar cosmetology industry with its "makeup magic" nor the distinguished dermatology profession with its ability to correct flaws we all wish we didn't have can cover the scars that lie deep within. Yet we expend countless dollars to add to our bag of tricks various shades, textures, and fabrics of the fashion industry with its memorable brand-name apparel, expensive accessories, and accouterments of glitz and glitter, none of which can remove the bruises of experience.

Not one of us is exempt from the residuals that certain memories and mismanagements have left deep inside the human soul. All of the artificial solutions only camouflage the shattered individuals beneath their elaborate masks. We need only take a tour of the homes of the rich and famous or stride into the urban areas, red-belt states, and Appalachian Mountains to know that while the tools are different, the issues remain the same, hidden beneath cowboy hats and Levis or the sagging jeans and overpriced sneakers of low-income kids: all cultures and classes pay exorbitant prices to cover what they cannot correct. Twenty-four-hour fitness centers hiss and turn until the wee hours of the morning to help us maintain the physiques we all like to see. But when all is stripped away, we live not with our image but with our realities, which neither treadmill nor eyeliner can erase.

Although the outer appearance may look fantastic, anyone who has ever dated can tell you that what you see isn't always what you get! Once you date the so-called beautiful people, you find out that not all that glitters is gold. This is not to say that the less aesthetic ones among us are any more whole or healed, because pain is without prejudice. It reaches us all.

This is why I'm happy that you are about to embark on a journey of wholeness! Author Touré Roberts has penned a powerful reminder to each and every one of us that no amount spent on that which surrounds us will deliver us from what mars that which is within us. This powerful, thought-provoking messenger is indeed the drum major who dares to beat the drum that leads us to the place where we can finally hear the sound that transforms us from the mundane to the miraculous. It is the inner life of those of us who march through life with half smiles and fully broken hearts to the dissonant sound of real regrets and mayhem that are Touré's focus. It is a less than merry band of life's participants he feels committed to lead into a place of harmony that they never thought they could successfully attain.

I first met Touré Roberts when he was courting my youngest daughter. I opened the door of my home with the skepticism that most fathers have when your daughter is talking too much about someone about whom you know too little. It is from this watchful perch I became a spectator and ultimately converted to the rhythm of his wisdom far beyond his years.

I pulled up a chair and dropped my glasses to the bridge of my nose to observe this young man who I thought on first blush was just another bag of britches and brawn. But on closer observation, I found that he has survived the vicissitudes of life with a gallantry and poetic cadence that don't seem to show the scars of a life filled with dangerous beginnings and less than perfect origins, and has emerged undaunted. As I watched and listened, prayed and pondered, I became more and more impressed with his insights and honesty, intrigue and curiosity from which his message of Wholeness is formulated. I eventually become so captivated and convinced, as I'm sure you will, that he is the perfect one to discuss wholeness with us.

Eventually, Touré went from suitor to groom. And me? Well, I traded my skeptical glare for a gaze of deep admiration. We have grown in our relationship, and I have evolved from doubter to Dad as I became a spiritual mentor and a father in the faith to this uniquely gifted individual. Although I originally met him as the guy who seemed "too good to be true," he quickly turned into a resource and I wondered how we ever did anything of consequence without him.

His story is captivating and his words transformative, and one would never guess from his peaceful presence and quiet tone the tempestuous ride Touré has taken to prepare himself for the task of drum major of a band of less than merry men and women. In his message you can hear the honest application of truth, coupled with the fact that he emerges from his dangerous beginnings having tried what he teaches and having partaken of what he now preaches to any who will listen and read his map to recovery. What is inspiring is his infectious love of people and his dedicated commitment to leading all those around him to that place of wholeness and tranquility at which he himself has arrived.

As I read through the early renderings of this riveting book, I could clearly see that Touré has discovered and delivered to all who will follow a path to wholeness that gets in the groove between theology and psychology with a lesson in the art of life, a lesson that neither theology nor psychology left to itself completely conveys. But with both studies, like drumsticks in the hands of a drummer, he beats out a rhythm that revives the weary and rejuvenates the disenfranchised.

By the time I finished this book, I felt as though I had been in the Underground Railroad with Harriet Tubman, leading slaves to freedom, or in South Africa watching Nelson Mandela and singing with the liberated in the aftermath of apartheid. Maybe it was written with the gentleness of Mother Teresa in Calcutta, feeding the trembling lips of a starving child. No, in fact, it was Touré Roberts, the man, the message, and the missive that left me thinking how vitally important this timely book would be in the hands of those who are secretly captive to the memories and agonies all of us are in some way exposed to.

Welcome to the freedom train to Wholeness. This book is not an expenditure of time or treasure; it is rather an investment in the innumerable possibilities all of us can attain if we decide to spend less on what surrounds us and more on what's within us. The returns on wholeness far exceed the investment. This is healing-in-a-bag for those of us who refuse to look like or live like where we came from. I present to some and introduce to others my son in faith and family, and the work and wealth of Touré Roberts' wholeness.

PREFACE: BECOMING WHOLE

From as far back as I can remember, I've had an unsettled spirit. I've been constantly on the move, looking for how things in my life could be bigger and better and how I could be wiser. I've always been searching for more, a trait I undoubtedly inherited from my mother.

My remarkable mother never let being a single parent with limited resources keep her from pursuing more in life. She refused to settle. She was determined to seek out the best that life had to offer us, and that's what she did. While I was growing up, I watched her rise from receptionist to executive and move from renting homes to buying them. In hindsight, I know that the changes happening in Mom's external life were directly related to what she was experiencing internally. It was her nonvisible transformation—the pursuit of a vibrant and healthy inner life—that fueled her external success. Mom had discovered the power of pursuing wholeness.

There isn't a subject that I am more passionate about—one that I want every person to understand before leaving earth—than the reality of wholeness. Throughout this book, we'll explore the deeper meaning of wholeness, but in the simplest terms, wholeness is the state of being complete. It means to be *unbroken*, having no cracks or missing parts that unhealthy and unprofitable fillers can occupy. Wholeness is the highest and healthiest version of any person, a version so awesome that to die before experiencing it would be one of life's greatest tragedies.

The process of becoming whole is like a perpetual heart, mind, and soul makeover, with a better you emerging with every cycle of growth. Cracks in your soul begin to mend and wrinkles in your spirit are smoothed out, revealing the masterpiece you were created to be. It doesn't matter if you're a single parent, successful businessperson, or celebrity. At the core, our issues are the same and the solution is the same— becoming whole. Wholeness is the greatest state of being this life offers, and we can all begin to pursue it right where we are.

In my role as pastor of a large church, I've witnessed this transformation up close and personal. But before watching people experience wholeness, I was witness to something else. In the early days of our church especially, I was puzzled by a recurring pattern I noticed in members of the congregation. At the time, we were drawing many up-and-coming actors, models, singers, and musicians. I was stunned by their talents, giftedness, and beauty; yet at the same time, I couldn't understand why so many were insecure, fearful, depressed, and unsuccessful. They did not lack talent or skill, yet they struggled to succeed and move forward in their lives.

After closely observing this, I realized something. Their instability was tied to hidden areas of brokenness in their lives. This brokenness was sabotaging not only their careers but also their relationships. As I got to know these people better, I recognized that their self-perception, and perception of life in general, was skewed and unhealthy. The irony was that most of these young artists had been full of hope and inspiration when they left home to pursue their careers. However, after getting to Los Angeles, they became discouraged, some nearly to the point of giving up.

It would be easy to surmise that the pressures and hard knocks of life in Hollywood brought on this brokenness, that the callous culture of show business was to blame. But pastoring these talented aspirants led me to a different conclusion. What became evident was that they were broken before they got here. It simply took the sometimes-cold-hearted environment of Hollywood to draw their brokenness to the surface.

I met beautiful supermodels who saw themselves as nothing but ugly and overweight. I witnessed brilliant people who were afraid to speak up because their brokenness told them they weren't smart enough to give input. I saw people trapped in abusive relationships because something told them they deserved the abuse and that life would not afford them anything better. Over the years, I came across countless stories like these, and there was one common denominator— some form of brokenness. Each person had broken areas within, creating broken paradigms and ultimately producing broken and unfulfilled lives.

Now, this is where you may begin to wonder if this book is for you. After reading some of these stories, you may think that you are in pretty good shape. However, even if you feel more whole than the people I described, make no mistake—none of us escape life's breakings. Whether you were teased as a child, were overlooked in your family, endured a divorce, or experienced any combination of the unlimited ways a person can be broken, life spares its rod on no one. Brokenness costs all of us something, and until we are made whole on every level, we live "leaking," some of us more than others. If brokenness never gets resolved over a lifetime, one person's small leak that goes untended for decades can cost that person significantly more than does the huge leak of a person who decides early on to pursue wholeness.

This book is about helping you address the leaks no matter where you are on your path. Bigger, better, wiser, and happier is waiting for you in the land of wholeness. Let's journey with each other, page by page, and together we'll be made whole.

PART 1

THINGS WE TELL OURSELVES THAT KEEP US FROM WHOLENESS

CHAPTER 1

"I THOUGHT I WAS WHOLE ALREADY"

This is a waste of time, I sighed to myself and reluctantly endured the relentless Los Angeles traffic to make a doctor's appointment—an appointment I felt was unnecessary. My persistent mother had been asking me for months to get a physical. She firmly believed I needed to be proactive about my health, regardless of how healthy I may have felt I was. For me, however, getting a checkup was the last thing on my mind.

I felt great and things in my life couldn't be better. I was an energetic socialite with a large network of friends. I was a top performer in the technology industry and had a robust pipeline filled with lucrative deals to be closed. I was making great money and had a solid five-year plan. I had a good rhythm going. The last place I wanted to be was at the doctor's office. Nevertheless, as a courtesy to my mom, I found myself pulling into a parking spot there and heading into the building.

The woman behind the counter checked me in and handed me a pen and a clipboard full of forms. The paperwork included a questionnaire with a long list of diseases and health conditions. As I checked off the no box next to each one, I remember gloating over how healthy I was, reinforcing to myself how unnecessary the doctor's visit was.

Soon a nurse escorted me to an examination room and took my vitals—pulse, temperature, respiration, and blood pressure. She smiled and said in an assuring tone that everything looked really good. She made a few notes in my file and told me that the doctor would be in to see me shortly. A few minutes later the doctor walked in, greeted me, flipped through my file, and confirmed the nurse's account of my healthy vital signs.

I felt relieved and thought my visit would soon come to an end. Everything had proven to be just fine, which meant I could get Mom off my back and officially add "good health" to the checklist of things going right in my life. Another slam dunk! But it turned out that the examination had merely scratched the surface. I learned that the most trustworthy diagnoses in life don't come from surface-level examinations. To get to the truth of the matter requires digging more deeply. In this case, digging more deeply required a blood draw. We had heard the testimony of my externals, but now it was time for my insides to take the stand.

After a few days, my blood results came in, and I was shocked by what they revealed. I was suffering from a condition that, if left untreated, would put me at risk for heart disease. It was a condition that could threaten my life. When it came to my health, things definitely were not as good as they appeared. I felt numb and confused. How could everything seem fine when in reality a train wreck was swiftly approaching? This tough news became the catalyst for change that affected not only how I approached my physical health but also how I approached my life.

It's easy to become so distracted in our efforts to create a life that we fail to consider whether we may have ailments that threaten the very life we are striving to create. For example, we might want to marry "the one" but fail to realize that until we become one within ourselves, happily ever after isn't likely going to happen. Or we might desire to be financially secure and don't have trouble earning money but somehow still end up living from paycheck to paycheck. Money slips right through our hands because something beneath the surface causes us to squander what we earn.

Could it be that sometimes you never achieve what you're striving for because a hidden issue is sabotaging you? Are you assuming you're living the best life possible when the truth is that undetected issues are working against the very best that life has to offer you?

I realize that these may be jarring questions, but just as I had to experience a rude awakening to change the trajectory of my life, perhaps you're due for a wake-up call as well. After years of counseling hundreds of "perfectly normal" people through frustrating circumstances that ultimately exposed deep under-the-surface issues, I believe we owe it to ourselves to make sure we don't go through life without taking inventory of who we are inside.

The great news is that having encouraged countless people to commit to specific disciplines, I've witnessed astounding results. I've seen people with fairly good and manageable lives experience a new dimension of existence they once didn't even believe was possible. I've witnessed others whose lives were in shambles experience life makeovers and find beauty and great treasure where they once saw only ruins. These people have experienced such dramatic transformations that who they once were now seems nearly unrecognizable to them.

I've got my own story of transformation to tell, but we'll get to that soon enough. For now, I want to return to what I learned following my doctor's visit: three life-changing principles that helped me to chart a new course.

1. NEVER OVERESTIMATE YOURSELF

We are often encouraged not to underestimate ourselves, and I believe in that wholeheartedly. Not underestimating yourself is about believing in yourself and your potential for greatness. There is more potential within us than we could ever fathom, and so we should never think little of ourselves or shrink back from pushing the boundaries of what we can achieve. At the same time, we can't be so sure of ourselves that we deceive ourselves. Failing to take an inner inventory could prove to be a great mistake with severe consequences.

Jesus made a provocative statement concerning self-examination: "They that are whole have no need of a physician" (Mark 2:17 ASV). It appears that Jesus is saying that a physician, someone who makes others whole, is relevant only to those who are sick. If you believe you are already whole, you have no need for the wholeness the doctor can bring. Is Jesus saying that only some people need to be made whole, or is he implying something different? Could it be that Jesus is really saying that people who mistakenly think they are whole close themselves off to the healing they don't realize they need?

It is difficult for most of us to see ourselves as we are. We all have blind spots that keep us from seeing what's going on beneath the surface. If we haven't learned how to be self-aware, our inner layers remain hidden from us. And living our best possible lives will elude us if we overestimate ourselves by assuming we are already living them.

Jesus doesn't let anyone off the hook when it comes to being whole. He understands our need to discover and pursue wholeness at every stage of life regardless of how well we may appear in our own eyes. Overestimating ourselves keeps us not only from becoming truly whole but also from experiencing the rich existence that comes only through wholeness.

2. PRIORITIZE YOUR INNER OVER YOUR OUTER

When I was a teenager, an elderly woman named Clara Jones attended our church. Clara always made it a point to dialogue with the young people and encourage us with kind words.

I remember this one exchange that she had with me nearly every time she saw me. It went something like this.

"Hi, Touré! You sure are a good-looking young man!"

Before I could get in a good blush, she followed up with, "Make sure you're just as handsome on the inside as you are on the outside." Her follow-up comment about my insides wasn't exactly deflating, but it certainly balanced the pride I felt when she paid the initial compliment.

"Yes, ma'am," I always modestly replied and continued on my way until our paths crossed again.

Mrs. Jones and I had that same exchange dozens of times, year after year. It got to the point that I was tempted to finish her thought for her. I always wondered if she'd forgotten we'd had that exact dialogue the last time we'd seen each other. Her words, although gracious and affirming, also challenged a deep part of me. It took years and a plethora of life lessons before I realized the powerful truth of her simple phrase: prioritize your inner life over your outer life, your inner success over your outer success, and your inner beauty over your outer beauty.

It's a truth our world desperately needs to hear. We live in a world obsessed with outer improvement. Cosmetic surgery in America has become a $13 billion dollar industry. There are more new fitness programs popping up than we can keep up with, each promising six-pack abs, toned arms, and lean thighs. Even high fashion has trickled down from the runways of Paris into the hallways of elementary schools as our youngsters are striving to be somebody, or at least to look like it. Our culture is fascinated with image and appearance like never before. Studies show that more than one out of three Americans are in debt, oftentimes living above their means to maintain some glamorous facade.

Technology and social media feed this obsession with externals. Why have a double chin when an app can remove it from that selfie you just took? And go ahead and slim down your waistline, bulk up your biceps, and lighten or darken your skin tone. If you alter your image to perfection, you'll no doubt be rewarded with "likes" from other users, which not only reinforces your need for their approval but makes it even harder to be who you really are. The irony is that oftentimes the people on the other end of those coveted affirmations are also approval seekers hiding behind altered images of their own. They too are seeking the almighty like for themselves. And so we find ourselves living in a culture that seeks instant affirmation based not on who we are inwardly but on who we can present ourselves to be outwardly. Mrs. Jones would not approve.

To avoid any misunderstanding, let me make one thing plain. I believe in taking pride in your appearance. I'd like to think I've got a slight knack for fashion myself. I also believe that being diligent in self-care is important. I live by this rule, and I teach it to my children and others. Without a doubt, how you present yourself in life is important. But today's desperate pursuit of approval based on outward appearances is causing a famine beneath the surface, and we neglect who we are inwardly to our peril.

There are two aspects to every human being: the ideal and the real. The ideal you is who you desire to be, who you strive to be, and sometimes who you pretend to be. It's the version you want others to see. It's the part of you that strives for all the likes. That's the ideal you.

The real you is much different. It's the you that lives beneath the surface. It's the most honest version of yourself. The real you is rarely known to others and, truth be told, is often little known even to yourself. It's the place where your flaws live—both known flaws and the ones that hide in your blind spots. It's the version of you that has been shaped by many factors, both positive and negative. This is the part of you that determines how you see and respond to circumstances. Much of what you experience in your outer life is the direct result of what is happening in the complex recesses of your inner life—the real you.

Hidden behind Mrs. Jones' simple encouragement, "Make sure you're just as beautiful on the inside as you are on the outside," is a priceless and powerful insight. She was no doubt familiar with this pearl of wisdom from the book of Proverbs: "Above every charge keep thy heart, for out of it are the outgoings of life" (Prov. 4:23 YLT).

The Hebrew word translated "heart" in this passage isn't referring to the physical heart in the center of your chest. It's speaking of the totality of your insides: your feelings, your will, and your intellect, all of which exist in the core of who you are. The point the proverb wants to make is that your outer life emanates from your inner life, and that means your inner life must be diligently understood, protected, and nurtured. This is the basis of wholeness. To experience wholeness, you must acknowledge your inner life, ensure its well-being, and pursue and preserve the healthiest version of the real you.

3. BE PROACTIVE, NOT PASSIVE, WHEN PURSUING WHOLENESS

My rude awakening after my doctor's visit stripped me of the luxury of being passive about my physical health. The message was loud and clear: physical health is nothing to take for granted. I know this isn't rocket science or even a profound epiphany for most of us. Even if we don't attend to it as well as we should, we already know that things like regular exercise and good nutrition are essential for health. However, many of us do need an epiphany when it comes to emotional and spiritual health. We still don't seem to understand that we need to be just as proactive about the health of our inner person as we are about the health of our body.

There are all sorts of reasons why most people might not prioritize the health of their inner person. For the most part, people can be divided into three groups: those who don't know, those who don't know what to do, and those who are afraid to act on what they know.

1. *Those who don't know.* These are well-meaning people who do the best they can in life but haven't awakened

to the truth that best begins from within. They take life as is and tend to adapt to their environment and circumstances rather than try to change them. They can't pursue wholeness because they have little to no understanding of what wholeness is. Their ignorance is their vice.

2. *Those who don't know what to do.* These people are often frustrated in life yet feel helpless to do anything about it. They want peace, happiness, and fulfillment but always seem to run into obstacles they can't overcome. They desire wholeness but don't know how to get there.

3. *Those who are afraid to act on what they know.* These people understand their need for wholeness and the effort needed to get there. However, they fail to pursue wholeness because they are held hostage by fear and are intimidated by the work required to achieve it. They want a better life but are afraid to get to the bottom of whatever prevents them from taking action. Wholeness is within their reach, but they are afraid to pay the cost.

You are reading this book for a reason. Perhaps you have never considered that you aren't already whole. It's possible that wholeness is a brand-new concept. If that's you, I get it; I was once there too. My prayer for you is that your eyes will be opened to the rich and rewarding life that becoming whole will afford you if you pursue it.

Wholeness is the highest and healthiest version of a person. It is like the character of "Wisdom" in Proverbs, who protects and watches over its subjects. "Wholeness" often calls me to change, to believe in the impossible, and to go beyond myself to become a greater me. As we journey through these pages together, I invite you to picture Wholeness as a Person who changed my life and who can change yours too.

Wholeness is going to require you to dig deep. You must be willing to visit places within yourself you may never have been and to enter rooms in your heart you've been afraid to go into, but don't worry. Wholeness is going to guide you, comfort you, encourage you, and cheer you on. Wholeness is excited that you've taken this first step. You've already begun to win. Now let's go farther.

CHAPTER 2

"IT'S NOT A BIG DEAL"

I never thought I'd be a pastor. I had no idea it was in the divine plan for me. I don't hail from a long line of ministers, nor did I ever have any early aspirations for ministry. If you had told me in my early twenties that I would one day be a spiritual leader, I would have laughed and asked you what you'd been smoking and inquired as to where I might get the same. The truth is, I didn't choose this path; this path chose me, and I am constantly floored with gratitude that it did.

One of the things I love most about being a pastor is having a front-row seat to what God is doing in people's lives. There is nothing more remarkable than witnessing the transformation of a human life. Maybe you understand what I'm talking about, because you've seen it too. It's the beauty of watching someone experience a complete life renovation and then enjoy the freedom to dream, soar, and accomplish things they never knew they were capable of. What makes this experience even more beautiful for me is when I get to be the vessel God uses to facilitate such a divine work. It's a tremendous honor and great reward that many of us pastors enjoy. And yet I have to admit that being a pastor comes with its share of challenges. The one that grieves me the most? Human complacency. It's an attitude of the heart that says, "I'm content with average. Wholeness? It's not a big deal."

There's nothing more challenging in my role as pastor than wanting more for people than they want for themselves. When that happens, my greatest gift—the ability to see the highest potential in a person—feels more like my greatest burden. The gift motivates me to invest in others as passionately as I invest in myself. Yet many times I end up feeling deflated and disappointed by those who choose complacency over progress. They express high aspirations in the empowering atmosphere of church service or a counseling session, but their lack of follow-through communicates what they're really thinking: *It's not a big deal. It's not exactly where I want to be, but I'll just accept life right where it is.*

MEDIOCRITY

What first comes to mind when you hear the word mediocrity? Chances are, whatever feels like mediocrity to you may not feel like mediocrity to someone else. Why? Because mediocrity is subjective. What looks mediocre to one person may look like achievement to another. And if we are pushing the boundaries of our own growth and potential, the achievements we reach in this season of life may feel like mediocrity in the next season. Allow me to illustrate with a personal story.

The latest addition to our family is our beautiful daughter Ella. When she was learning to walk, she began by standing for long periods of time without our help. Each time she stood up on her own, we enthusiastically applauded her and cheered, "Yay, Ella!" This really boosted her confidence, causing her to smile radiantly and wait for the next opportunity to be praised. Her sense of what was acceptable was formed by our applause and affirmations.

After a few weeks of this, she began to applaud herself. When she stood on her own, she clapped her tiny hands together without any prompting from us. Her standard for excellence had been shaped by our praise, and consequently she praised herself by that same measure. This meant that in addition to building Ella's confidence, our affirmations also established her parameters for what was good, appropriate, and acceptable.

All of this was fine while Ella was learning to walk, but I hope we aren't still applauding her for standing up when she's four or ten or sixteen. And I hope she won't be satisfied with applauding herself, for the same reasons. When she has the potential to walk, run, leap, and dance, why would she ever settle for merely standing up?

As parents, our job is to encourage our children throughout life and to help them grow. That includes creating an environment within our home that gives them confidence and allows them to flourish. However, it also means equipping our children to venture outside the home in ways that will challenge and stretch them. If we fail in this regard, the same nurturing environment that first affirmed them will end up putting borders on their potential.

Our views about what makes an effort mediocre or commendable are the byproduct of what we've been exposed to, and those standards change depending on how much we've accomplished. Have you ever found yourself feeling like a rock star in one environment but then feeling like a total incompetent in a new one? What's exemplary in one context becomes basic in the next. This is normal when you're committed to progress. What was once your ceiling becomes your floor. That's why it's important that we never allow ourselves to be complacent about our growth in and toward wholeness. We have to keep challenging and stretching ourselves so we don't fall short of our potential.

HALFWAY UP THE MOUNTAIN

We typically associate the word mediocre with terms like ordinary, average, undistinguished, and middle-of-the-road. However, when I did a little digging, I discovered that the linguistic origins of the word actually suggest something slightly different and more profound.

The word mediocre originates from the Latin *mediocris*, which is composed of two other Latin words: *medi*, which means "mid," and *ocris*, meaning "rugged mountain." When we put those two words together, the literal translation is "mid rugged mountain," or halfway up the mountain. That image provides a very different perspective on what the word mediocre really means. It suggests that being mediocre is not just being ordinary or average. It means that someone who is mediocre hasn't reached the peak of his or her potential but has instead stalled out at the halfway point. And it wasn't too long ago that I came to understand how easy it is to stall out halfway up the mountain.

By the age of forty, I felt like I had made good strides in reaching some mountaintops in my life. I had founded a church from scratch that in just twelve years had more than three thousand people attending each week. We also streamed our services online and had tens of thousands of viewers from around the world. I had signed a contract with a prominent publisher, and my first book would soon be hitting the shelves. Even better, my success with the church led to a meeting with a beautiful woman named Sarah whom I married just nine months later. Talk about a mountaintop experience!

In addition to love, friendship, and children, Sarah also brought two unexpected gifts into my life—her parents! From our first meeting, Thomas Dexter and Serita Ann Jakes loved me like their own son. Mrs. Jakes lavished me with affirmation and meaningful Christmas and housewarming gifts, and she regularly expressed her appreciation for the way I cared for her daughter. Mr. Jakes, more widely known on every continent as Bishop T. D. Jakes, embraced me warmly as well, although he did spend quite a bit of time checking me out first. As he would say, he had to "kick the tires" and "shake the tree" a little to make sure there were no hidden surprises. He wanted to ensure that the man who would be caring for his daughter had the capacity to do so. Eventually, he took me in, but only after the CIA cleared my background. Just kidding—I think.

Dad Jakes and I have developed an incredible relationship. The wisdom, guidance, and knowledge afforded me through our friendship is priceless, but perhaps the biggest gift he's given me was removing the veil of mediocrity from my eyes. From the beginning of our relationship, he affirmed two things in me: what I had already accomplished and what I had yet to accomplish. He helped me to see that I was only halfway up my mountain, not standing near the top.

In hindsight, I can see that there was little around me challenging me to go farther. All I could hear in the environment around me was applause. I'd built a successful church that in terms of attendance, resources, recognition, and influence had surpassed every church I'd been exposed to as I was growing up. I was the first in my family to publish a book and had gone much farther in life than my father had before he passed away. Compared to most people I had grown up with in the inner city, I had shattered every threshold for success. From the graffitied walls of Watts, where I grew up, to the hills overlooking the city that I now call home, the only sound I heard was applause. The people around me were applauding and, like my little daughter Ella, I was applauding myself. But Dad Jakes' mentorship and motivation revealed to me something I didn't know about applause. It is often deceiving.

My accomplishments were indeed worthy of applause,

but not the type of applause that says, "Congratulations, you've arrived! Welcome to the mountaintop!" Instead it was the kind of true applause meant to do what Dad Jakes did for me—affirm what I had accomplished but also remind me of what I had yet to achieve. This kind of applause says, "Great job getting halfway up the mountain! Now keep going!" At the time, everyone in my world was cheering about my halfway point, but Wholeness was calling me higher up the mountain toward my potential.

Wholeness had conspired with Dad, causing him to affirm my accomplishments but more importantly to speak to my potential. Wholeness always calls you higher and constantly looks for a way to expose you to greater possibilities. Wholeness wants to stretch your mind by giving you a vision of what is possible, hoping you will have the faith and fortitude to do whatever is required to keep climbing your mountain. Wholeness won't climb your mountain for you, nor will he force you up the mountain. All he will do is extend the invitation, promise the beauty of the mountaintop, inspire the strength needed to ascend, and rejoice over who you become in the process.

When Wholeness calls you higher, you will have to resist the gravitational pull of complacency, or what I sometimes call "sameness." The journey forward is an ascent. It will always be far easier for you to stay the same than it will be for you to do the work needed to climb farther up your mountain. You have to overcome the downward pull of sameness. Even when your desire for wholeness is strong and you feel excited and optimistic about the future, your natural human tendencies are inclined to revert back to what has always been. You've got to fight for your progress and resist the forces within that resist change.

I've seen this downward pull of sameness with people who have come to me for counseling. Their circumstances prompted their desire for change, but their lack of resolve kept them from doing anything differently. In the presence of knowledge and wisdom they saw the light, but when they returned to the environment in which they needed to make a change, they lost their fortitude and their plans dissolved. On the other hand, I have also counseled others who were so committed to the vision of wholeness for their lives that they submitted to the process, fought the pressures of gravity, and experienced the new life that was waiting for them on the other side. In the pursuit of wholeness, we always have a choice—to give in to the pressure of sameness or to draw on God's power to keep climbing.

SMALLSVILLE OR DESTINYLAND?

I've got a question for you: Have you identified your greatest fear? I know what mine is, and I want to share it with you, though it may not be what you expect. It has nothing to do with dying or losing everything I've amassed. It's not even the fear of losing loved ones, although that would be devastating. My greatest fear is this: not reaching my potential in life. Although I've written and preached about disciplines for overcoming many fears in life, this is one fear I give you full permission to have.

Your potential is so critical and valuable that the idea of *not* fully reaching it should alarm you. It alarms me unlike anything else. The agony of wondering what I may have left on the table in life is too much to bear. Did I do everything I possibly could to avoid mediocrity, to avoid stalling out and settling for life halfway up my mountain? Did I play the hand I was dealt well, or did I stall while complaining about my cards? Is contentment with my accomplishments to date deceiving me into thinking I have reached my mountaintop, or am I continuing to heed the call that beckons me upward? Have I allowed the applause of my environment to drown out the faint voice of Wholeness whispering, "There's more"?

As those who are being made whole, we must regularly ask ourselves these questions. They help us take the blinders off and see where we're really at in life. Potential is often described as something that must be reached. But the word reach has two meanings: arriving at the destination and also stretching ourselves to get there.

You may ask, "If my potential is always out in front of me, always higher on the mountain, how will I even know when I reach it?" Here's the truth: for most of your life, you probably won't know. Potential will be always beyond what you thought. That's why you and I must always keep reaching. I sometimes describe this as resisting the temptation to settle in Smallsville and instead making the decision to climb up to Destinyland. As we've already noted in our discussion of mediocrity, Smallsville and Destinyland are always changing. What was once Destinyland for you becomes Smallsville as you climb higher up the mountain of potential.

I've got another question for you: Where would you say you are living right now? In Smallsville, where you know your way around, are known by everyone, and have nothing to challenge you? Or in Destinyland, the scary place where you feel like a stranger but are comforted by the presence and the promises of the God who travels with you? If you've been living in Smallsville, I encourage you to move out and hit the upward trail. Destinyland is waiting for you, and it's worth any cost you have to pay to get there.

It's important to keep one thing in mind while moving up your mountain, and that is patience. Challenging yourself to grow is not the same thing as beating yourself up. You must be your own best friend and cheerleader (not your own worst critic) on your way up the mountain. When Wholeness calls you higher, his tone is not one of disappointment or disapproval. Instead he speaks with the voice of encouragement and confidence, and he wants you to believe in your ability to rise to the occasion. Wholeness never calls you *beyond* your ability; he calls you *according* to it.

Are you ready to grow? Do you hear Wholeness calling you by name and inviting you to more? Climbing the mountain will take work, and it will take some time, but God has equipped you with everything you need to take your next step. The life waiting for you on the other side of transformation is a very big deal indeed, and more than worth the effort required to reach it.

CHAPTER 3

"I'M OKAY"

Up to this point, we've dealt with two out of the three most common things we tell ourselves that keep us from wholeness: "I thought I was whole already" and "It's not a big deal." However, I am convinced that nothing we tell ourselves poses more of a threat to our wholeness than the phrase "I'm okay." Too often these words effortlessly roll off our tongues as a reflexive response to anything that questions our strength or our ability to have it all together. *I may be devastated, but I'm okay. I'm experiencing tremendous pain, but I'm okay. Someone I love hurt me deeply, but I'm okay.* Maybe you've said words like these to yourself. I know I have. I routinely said them to myself until a difficult circumstance several years ago forced me to finally admit, "I'm *not* okay."

It was just a few weeks away from Father's Day, and I wanted to do something special for my dad. My biological father and I didn't have the best relationship. I never truly felt close to him. My early childhood memories of my father are vague to nonexistent. If it weren't for a few photos I managed to collect over the years, I wouldn't have known he was even around when I was young. I have more vivid memories of times with my dad from my adolescence, as I can recall him making several trips to our home to pick me up for the weekend.

My father was a strict disciplinarian, and I dreaded weekend visits with him, sometimes to the point of tears. He was hard on me, and I was afraid of him. It was in stark contrast to the love, nurture, and affirmation I experienced with my mom. I lived in fear of making simple mistakes in front of him, because of the scorn and the ridicule I would undoubtedly receive. I can still remember how angry he became one time when I spilled milk while trying to pour it into a bowl of cereal. He reacted as if I'd done it intentionally, as if there were no possible way a small child who was paying attention could ever miss the bowl.

I learned to walk on eggshells around him to avoid arousing his temper and the piercing words that would fly out of his mouth when he was displeased. The fear of upsetting him only increased my anxiety, as well as the odds that I would make even more mistakes that angered him. As I grew older, spilling milk wasn't so much an issue anymore, but my father still found ways to call my life into question or to reiterate his vision of success for my life, regardless of how different it was from my own.

The older I got and the more accomplished I became, the more our relationship seemed to improve. As my success became more evident and undeniable, his critiques seemed to lessen. He still found occasions to throw darts of inadequacy my way, but I learned to disregard them. I had adopted this principle from the Ten Commandments: "Honor your father and your mother" (Deut. 5:16). I was counting on the corresponding promise that doing so meant things would go well with me. That verse helped me and called me to take the high road in our relationship, regardless of whether I thought my father's actions deserved honor. I believed that I should honor him not because of how he treated me but simply because he was my father—imperfect and all. I was determined to think the highest thoughts concerning him and also sought to understand him better. I told myself that, considering the difficulties of his own upbringing, he was doing the best he could by me.

In anticipation of this particular Father's Day, I decided to do something special for my dad. I knew he liked deep-sea fishing, so I decided to coordinate a trip to celebrate him on Father's Day. This was a big step for me. I loved my father, but we hadn't gotten past the awkwardness of spending any real length of time together. On this trip, we'd be on a boat together for several hours, miles away from shore—this should give you a good idea of how much I was really putting myself out there. Nevertheless, in the name of honor, I picked up the phone and extended the invitation.

Dad seemed a little surprised by my offer, but he accepted the invitation and told me to keep him posted with the details. His positive response was a huge relief to me, and I felt a sense of accomplishment. Just presenting an idea to him that was acceptable—without critique—was a victory. Having it be something that honored him and would ultimately please him gave me a sense that things were beginning to turn around in our relationship. I felt as if this part of my life was finally making the kind of positive turn I'd experienced in so many other areas.

Unfortunately, I was wrong. Things didn't exactly work out as I had planned.

Two weeks later I phoned my father to give him the details of our trip. I was excited to have worked out the logistics, the trip was set, and all we needed to do was show up. However, I didn't get the enthusiastic response I had expected. The response I got was jarringly familiar.

"I've made other plans for Father's Day," Dad said. "It's your fault this isn't going to work out, because you didn't give me the details sooner."

I was speechless. And yet I told myself I shouldn't have been surprised. After all, it wasn't unlike my father to be erratic and critical. He didn't have much of a filter for what he said, nor did he show his sensitive side very often. I told myself I should be perfectly okay with Dad just being Dad in this scenario, as he had been in so many others. I even told myself that I was okay. But I wasn't okay, and the accumulated brokenness from our relationship was about to come crashing down on me.

IT'S OKAY *NOT* TO BE OKAY

As Father's Day approached, my mother asked me how plans for the fishing trip were shaping up. I told her that Dad had backed out but that it was okay because I really didn't want to go in the first place. Later, when a close friend asked about the trip, I was beginning to give a similar answer when I felt overcome by a deep emotion I had trouble identifying. The feeling was both unfamiliar and familiar. Something that had been buried within me was rising to the surface, and it was no longer going to be quiet.

To be honest, it felt like there was a screaming monster inside me that had suddenly been roused. This intruder beneath the surface was now setting off alarm bells that reverberated throughout every part of me. I tried to pray the intruder away and even tried to distract myself from it, but it wouldn't leave. This unstoppable force was disrupting my life, and I could not shake it.

With Father's Day just around the corner, I finally admitted that what was going on inside me would not simply go away. My peace was gone, my thoughts were fragmented, and to make matters worse, it was now Sunday morning, and in less than two hours I would stand before my congregation for the first of our two Sunday morning services with an enormous problem: I had nothing to say. Whatever this monster within me was, it cut off the flow of love and clarity I relied on week in and week out to prepare and deliver my messages to the congregation.

I felt overwhelmed with anxiety, but I was trying very hard to keep it all together. I was terrified to confront what was inside me. It was rage and pain and grief, and I didn't want to deal with any of it. If I took a real look at it—if I truly locked eyes with this monster—I wasn't sure I would come out of the encounter in one piece. I didn't know who I would become or what my life would look like if I lost the fight. I reasoned it would be better for me to function through my dysfunction until I had the wherewithal to handle it, but now I was up against the clock. The weekend messages I gave to the church were built on personal openness and transparency, and I knew I couldn't hide what I was going through beneath the surface. I was trapped.

As I stepped into the shower, I was exhausted, confused, and out of options. And yet somewhere in my heart I heard the whisper of a loving voice. *It's okay not to be okay.* In that moment, everything seemed to shift into slow motion, and my heart began to shift as well. Those whispered words were the divine key that released me from the shackles of fear and numbness.

It's okay not to be okay. As the warm water washed over me, those gentle healing words washed through me. I let go of my need to have it all together and surrendered to a process I knew would lead me toward wholeness. I also knew it would require facing the monster within. A newfound vulnerability came over me, and I began to sob uncontrollably. For the first time, I allowed myself to feel the emotion I'd buried when Dad told me he'd made other plans for Father's Day. The monster that rose up in me that day was Hurt, and its name was well deserved. *It's okay not to be okay.* I let it all go and gave myself permission to cry.

Standing in the shower that morning, I cried about the phone call with my dad, but it was actually a thirty-year-old cry—and long overdue. Somewhere along the way, I learned to stuff my emotions and to anesthetize the pain of rejection by telling myself, "I'm okay," even when I wasn't. The monster within was an accumulation of all the unprocessed feelings I'd buried over the years every time I felt rejected by my father. As I cried, my hurt erupted like a slow-motion volcano, and yet as messy as it was, I felt a healing relief with each sob.

We are never okay when we pretend that hurt doesn't hurt. Hurt always needs to be acknowledged and addressed. It doesn't just disappear, no matter how deeply we bury it or how much we try to convince ourselves we're okay in spite of it. When we fail to process our pain in a healthy way, it becomes ill-processed by default, deepening the damage of the original wound. That's what happens when the unhealthy layers of denial under which we bury our hurt stand in the way of our wholeness. What I experienced that morning in the shower was a cracking open of those layers. As my defenses crumbled, the light and hope of wholeness illuminated my pain and began to heal a wound I had been avoiding and denying for decades.

HURT, ANGER, AND PRIDE

I experienced a life-changing breakthrough that morning not simply because I was able to identify and address the hurt living beneath the surface but also because I discovered the unhealthy pattern that led me to repeatedly deny the pain.

It's one thing to be sick and then get healed. It's another to recognize how you got sick in the first place so you can avoid getting sick again. As I began the process of healing, I discovered the unique relationship between hurt, anger, and pride and how this destructive trio had worked aggressively against my wholeness and stifled my progress in life. Let me explain the connection.

To begin, it's important to understand something about who we are beneath the surface. Your inner person (what I described in chapter 2 as the real you) is the most delicate and sensitive part of you. Unlike your outer, physical self, your inner self can't be protected by layers of clothing. You can't bundle up your insides with the emotional equivalent of jackets, scarves, and caps to protect it from harsh environments. That means your inner person is wide open and subject to harm from any number of hostile elements in our world that threaten its wholeness. Three of the most common threats include:

- Being treated in a way that is debasing
- Being ridiculed with piercing and diminishing words
- Being unseen or unrecognized

All of these threats to wholeness have something in common—they are devaluing. And there is perhaps nothing more traumatizing to the human spirit than feeling devalued. It cuts to the core because God created human beings to be loved and valued. We're born with a fundamental need to be loved as is, with no strings attached. We are desperate for it and at times will do anything to try to find that kind of acceptance and care.

When we experience something that deprives us of the love and value we crave, the result is hurt, which is traumatizing to our inner person. Hurt is so traumatizing that most of us do everything in our power to avoid it. And if we can't avoid it, we try to manage it by transferring that pain into a secondary emotion such as anger. While hurt is the primary emotion, anger arises in response to the hurt in order to help us distance ourselves somewhat from the pain.

Anger is where we live when we are running from the reality of the hurt. In my case, the hurt that came from my father's rejection was anchored to a question: Am I good enough? I couldn't face the reality of the hurt because I was afraid I'd have to answer that question. What if I wasn't good enough? That thought was unbearable, especially to a spirit that was already wounded. And so my inner defense mechanism kicked in, and the hurt became anger.

The transition from hurt to anger is how that vulnerable inner person attempts to regain control after experiencing the shock of hurt. Anger is the perfect refuge because it takes the power away from the one who wounded us and places the narrative about the hurt within our own sphere of control. Anger puts every possibility of wrongdoing or inadequacy concerning the hurt away from ourselves and onto the one from whom the hurt came. The one who wounded is entirely at fault; the one who was hurt is entirely innocent. Although this emotional transfer to anger may offer temporary relief from the hurt, in the long run it causes more damage, and here's why.

When anger follows hurt, the anger is contrived. The true and primary feeling is hurt. Hurt will never be healed by anger. Being made whole after hurt requires an authentic encounter with the pain you are feeling. Burying and denying hurt only creates more dysfunction. Wholeness collaborates only with truth. He does not work in conjunction with dysfunctions we convince ourselves we need in order to remain functional. It takes courage and vulnerability to look hurt in the face and allow Wholeness to not only reveal the truth to you but lead you through the healing process. When we choose instead to shrink back from pursuing wholeness, we end up covering our hurt and anger with yet another layer, which is pride.

Pride is perhaps the most problematic mindset because it tries to masquerade as healing. It mimics wholeness by claiming all is well. Pride convinces us to deny being hurt because according to pride, hurt is something only the weak experience, and weak is the last thing we ever want to be. We might even deny being angry because pride leads us to believe that being angry is a loss of control. And so we smile and say, "I'm doing great" or "I don't care" or "It doesn't really matter," when in fact we aren't doing great, we do care, and it does really matter. In the process, we close ourselves off from the possibility of wholeness because our pride refuses to acknowledge that anything is broken. Pride is a tough layer to penetrate but, as I experienced in my own healing journey, when the wall of pride breaks down, unprecedented healing begins to flow.

SAFETY AND VULNERABILITY

My healing began the moment my trusted friend asked me how the fishing trip with my father was shaping up. Up to that point, I was living in the layer and mindset of pride. When my father rejected the fishing trip, I was disappointed and hurt. Not wanting to acknowledge the hurt, I quickly moved to anger, and then to pride. I was in denial and completely out of touch with what was going on inside me. It happened so seamlessly, so quietly beneath the surface, that I had no idea it had taken place.

However, when my friend asked about the trip, my wall of pride was penetrated. Pride, although stubborn, can be penetrated and surrendered if we feel safe. Remember, in situations such as these, pride is a vain attempt to protect our inner person from pain. Deep down, we all want to be made whole, but we won't reveal our brokenness to people or environments that will abuse our vulnerability. However, if an environment is perceived as safe, our inner person has an opportunity to set aside pride. When we feel safe, we can respond to the rare opportunity to be authentic because we trust we will not be judged, diminished, or devalued. There was something about my friend that created enough sense of safety that my wall of pride cracked and I was finally able to acknowledge that there was something broken beneath the surface.

As I stood sobbing in the shower that Sunday morning, desperately grasping for whatever I could use to hide my vulnerability, my wall of pride crumbled. *It's okay not to be okay.* It was the voice of Wholeness. I knew I was safe. Wholeness was giving me permission to be vulnerable and to trust that all my broken pieces could be put back together again, perhaps even better than before. And it ironic that this encounter that required an inner nakedness happened in the shower, a place that requires an outer nakedness. Both the symbolism and reality of my breakthrough were mind-boggling.

I was a changed man after that encounter. I went to church that morning and laid it all on the table. I was transparent about my experience with my father and the breakthrough that followed. That day, I preached a message about vulnerability that some have said is the most powerful message I've ever given. Afterward scores of people with tears flowing down their cheeks flocked to the altar for prayer. Grown men and women let down their guard, becoming as openhearted and vulnerable as young children. The entire congregation experienced the power of receiving permission to not have it all together. It was a beautiful exchange—brokenness for wholeness—and we all went home that day not perfect but undeniably better. As a church family, we were led farther up the mountain of our potential. My sermon title, which you already may have guessed, was "It's Okay Not to Be Okay." I'm sure Wholeness didn't mind me borrowing the phrase.

As we continue this challenging ascent to wholeness, I invite you to pause for a moment and reflect. Consider the layers we discussed—hurt, anger, pride—and ask yourself this important question: "Have I been honest with myself and others about hurt I have experienced?" Take a moment and think about it. Do others accuse you of being angry? If so, is there some unprocessed hurt beneath the anger? Do you often feel the need to appear to have it all together? Do you smile and say you're okay when deep down you know you're not? All it takes is a willingness to be vulnerable, and your life can be changed. Be brave in this moment and take a real good look. As you do, remember this: Wholeness is with you.

PART 2

THE TRUTH SHALL
SET YOU FREE

CHAPTER 4

MEET BROKENNESS

Since marrying my wife, Sarah, a southern girl, I've picked up a few country sayings. I love how they pack so much wisdom into just a few words. Like this one: "Even a broken clock is right twice a day." Think about it. There's a whole world of wisdom in that simple statement! What it means to me is that just because something works some of the time doesn't mean it can be relied on all of the time. Even a clock we rely on for accuracy can be wrong, and if we look at it only at certain times, we'll have no idea it's broken. Unless we are paying close attention, the brokenness of the clock will elude us. And the same principle applies to our inner lives. Just because a few areas of our lives may appear to be working well does not mean our lives are well. We have to pay close attention to our inner lives, or our brokenness will elude us.

Up to this point, we've talked about the kinds of things we tell ourselves that keep us from experiencing wholeness, but now it's time to take an even closer look at what lies behind all those statements, which is our brokenness.

WHAT'S WRONG WITH YOU?

One of the things that intrigues me about brokenness is that it seems like only a small number of people consider themselves to be broken in any way. However, the majority of people who don't consider themselves broken will acknowledge that they aren't perfect and make mistakes. How is it that most people will admit to imperfection but reject the notion of being broken? Are mistakes and shortcomings not evidence of at least some degree of brokenness in our lives? If our mistakes do not come from our brokenness, then where do our mistakes come from? Are we like broken clocks, so content with being spot-on twice a day that we are blinded to what our brokenness may be costing us the other hours of the day? The answer seems obvious, and for me that's the scary part. It's not what I've got worked out and operating well that keeps me up at night. It's what is yet to be made whole that concerns me.

When Sarah and I were in the early months of our courtship, the time had come for me to meet her father to discuss my interest in his daughter. It was the first time Mr. Jakes and I had ever sat down together, and once my nervousness subsided, it proved to be a heartfelt and meaningful talk. After discussing a series of questions and concerns—which I presumed I had answered satisfactorily—we seemed to be winding down our conversation. But my soon-to-be father-in-law had masterfully waited until the end of our discussion to ask me his most important question. With a piercing gaze that reached right into my soul, Mr. Jakes said, "Touré, I know what's right with you. That all looks good. But tell me, what's *wrong* with you?" It was a brilliant question—one I am certain to ask anyone seeking my blessing to marry one of our kids. In all my years, I had never been asked such a thing by anyone. Fortunately, it was a question I'd already learned to ask myself, so it wasn't hard to answer.

So tell me, what's wrong with you? Could you have readily responded to Mr. Jakes' question? How willing and able are you to acknowledge that there may be broken areas in your life? If you want to be whole, you have to understand, address, and ultimately surrender your brokenness on the altar of wholeness. And there is no shame in being broken. You didn't choose your brokenness; your brokenness chose you.

SMALL CRACKS OF BROKENNESS

We all come into this world with at least a crack when we are born. Those before us were born into brokenness, and those before them the same. The brokenness you inherit is not your fault, but it is very much your responsibility to overcome it. Why? Because if your brokenness is left unchecked, it will steal from you. Unacknowledged brokenness is like having a robber within, a thief intent on stealing the promising future you've been trying to lay hold of. When you take two steps toward wholeness, brokenness seeks to sabotage that progress by moving you two steps back.

Here's another way to think of it. Brokenness is like being overtaxed in life. There is a legitimate amount of tax we all must pay to cover the costs of living in our country. But imagine finding out that you have been paying significantly more than you need to—for years or even decades. Painful, right? That's exactly what brokenness does. It imposes a "broken tax"—a tax you wouldn't have to pay if you were whole in certain areas.

Is it possible that brokenness in your life is costing you far more than you realize? What if brokenness is stealing from you at this very moment? What would you do if you discovered that peace, love, progress, and even finances were all going out the back door of your life because brokenness has been embezzling your blessings for years? The brutal truth? It is entirely possible. Brokenness is just as committed to your not reaching your mountaintop of potential as Wholeness is to your getting there.

So the question we have to ask ourselves is, "If brokenness is so costly, why is it so challenging for us to acknowledge?" In my view, it comes down to two things: pride and blind spots. Pride is what allows us to admit we aren't perfect but prevents us from acknowledging brokenness. For the most part, imperfection is an acceptable norm in the human experience. You'll find the phrase "nobody's perfect" in everything from song lyrics and movie lines to social media posts and poor excuses from cheating lovers. Because imperfection is largely accepted, it escapes the requirement of change. It gives us an easy way out of our mistakes without the mandate for improvement. To be broken, however, is a different story.

Brokenness requires fixing, and pride refuses to admit that there is anything at all to fix.

Blind spots are just what they sound like—obstructions that keep us from seeing our own brokenness. One of the hardest things for us to see clearly and completely is ourselves. We are aware of most of what is in front of us but little of what is within us. We all have an idea of who we are, but only from a limited perspective—our own. This predicament is similar to the blind spots we have with our physical eyes. Our eyes are in the front of our heads and enable us to see what is directly in front of us. We can turn our head to the left and to the right and up and down, which means our viewing range covers, at best, a 180-degree view. This means that at any given moment, there are another 180 degrees we are not seeing. Even with the best eyesight, there will always be blind spots, sometimes significant ones. Brokenness rarely makes a formal introduction but rather hides and even thrives in our blind spots.

What makes our brokenness even harder to detect is that we have learned how to function with dysfunction. It's like using a crutch for a broken foot; as long as you have the crutch, you can still get around. That doesn't mean your foot is any less broken, but you might convince yourself that it's fine because, hey, you're still getting from one place to another, right? But the more functional we are with our dysfunction, the greater our self-deception. Why? Because we equate being functional with being fine. That may work for a while, but not forever. One day, the painful truth that all is not well will bring everything to a screeching halt.

FROM SMALL CRACKS TO CHASMS

As I mentioned earlier, we all come into this world with a crack or two, which is some degree of brokenness. We didn't choose it, but it is our reality. Then as we live in the world, we acquire a few more cracks, and the ones we already have deepen, sometimes into painful chasms. And that is the definition of brokenness. It means to be divided or split from within. We might acquire these cracks and splits in any number of ways. Here are just a few.

Generational brokenness. This is the brokenness we inherit from parents, grandparents, and even many generations before them. This could include domestic violence, alcoholism, or some other form of addiction. Because these issues were never addressed, they live on and perpetuate the cycle of brokenness from one generation to the next.

Social brokenness. We live in a broken world, which means there is brokenness in our culture at large, the subcultures we are exposed to, and the social systems that shape the way we relate to one another. Examples include poverty, racism, and sexism.

Personal brokenness. This is the brokenness we experience when we are devalued or traumatized. Examples include verbal, physical, and sexual abuse, as well as rejection and abandonment.

All of these forms of brokenness complicate and deepen our foundational brokenness. When brokenness is allowed to reign, it accumulates in layers—brokenness on top of brokenness. And then things get really complicated, because we inevitably attempt to heal our brokenness in ways that only produce more brokenness.

Take, for instance, a young woman whose father never affirmed her value when she was a child. As she enters her teen years, she feels a deep hunger for male attention and validation. Her father's rejection created a wide crack beneath the surface, and now anything that resembles affirmation by a man feels like the healing she's so hungry for. She's aware that men notice her figure, and she begins to play to their attention. She wears clothes that accentuate her breasts and bottom because it gets her more attention. The attention becomes like a drug, and she not only needs it but needs more of it and stronger doses of it to get the same effect. She alters her strut to draw attention to herself and posts revealing and seductive photos on social media.

Up to this point, it feels like she's been getting what she wants and needs, but now she's beginning to see there are complications that come along with the attention. The attention feeds her need for affirmation, but she knows that the men she's attracting don't want her for her; they only want her body parts. Her realization is a flash of truth that could lead her toward wholeness, but it's also a threat—she'd have to let go of vying for attention. Because she is so desperate to ease the pain of her brokenness, she exchanges the truth for the momentary filling of the void.

Eventually, the stakes get higher. Now the men want not only to look but also to touch. Not long ago, this would have been unthinkable to her, but her sense of self-worth has been gradually degraded with each compromise she has made for the attention. So she yields to one man's advances and now has offered not only her self-esteem but also her body on the altar of brokenness. The result? More brokenness. Guilt and shame widen the gap that started as a crack of rejection. Now it is a wide chasm that only an experience with wholeness can truly heal. But it doesn't stop there. She feels so overwhelmed by pain and shame and guilt that she must find an escape from it all. Drugs and alcohol promise the relief she's looking for, which only piles on more layers of brokenness.

Do you see how unacknowledged brokenness is robbing this young woman? And how her attempts to heal her brokenness on her own terms only make things worse? To one degree or another, the dynamics in her story are ones we all share, and the stakes are just as high for us. The sooner we recognize and acknowledge our brokenness, the sooner we can experience healing and wholeness.

RECOGNIZING BROKENNESS

As I mentioned earlier, recognizing brokenness is challenging —especially when pride and blind spots get in the way—but it is entirely possible. I'm going to briefly walk through three steps you can take. If you put them into practice regularly, it will be very difficult for brokenness to hide from you.

Step 1: Acknowledge That You Are Broken

This step takes humility and a commitment to self-examination. Set aside your pride and admit that you have blind spots. Say to yourself, "Although I may be functioning well in some areas, I won't use those as an excuse to avoid dealing with brokenness in other areas." This does not mean you have to beat yourself up or put yourself down. You need to think highly of yourself, just not so highly that you miss the brokenness that lurks low. When you acknowledge that you are broken, you are actually valuing yourself by eliminating any possibility of self-sabotage. You are putting the thief of brokenness on notice: no more stealing allowed.

Step 2: Follow the Pain

Where does your life hurt? Pain comes in many forms, including insecurity, envy, depression, anxiety, anger, loneliness, and low self-esteem. If you've been functioning with dysfunction for a long time, you may have become numb to the pain or think it's normal. But it's not normal, and you need to be healed. Don't turn a deaf ear to your inner person, the voice that says, "I'm hurting. This is hard. I need help." That's how you begin to develop the discipline of being self-aware. You listen and you acknowledge—to yourself and to others—when your inner person is experiencing discomfort or pain. Pain is a gift in this regard. Just as clues help detectives solve crimes, pain points us to what needs to be healed. If we recognize pain and respond to it properly by tracing it to its source, we are well on the road to wholeness. New life will spring up where brokenness once lived.

Step 3: Trust Outside Eyes

If you have blind spots, what do you need? Another set of eyes that can see what you cannot. Invite trusted friends to lend you their eyes. People close to you likely see things in you that you can't. No one wakes up in the morning and says, "Today I'm going to be an arrogant, selfish, insensitive human being." And yet we encounter people like this every day. It's easy to notice it in others, but it's difficult to recognize it in ourselves. So you need people in your life who will tell you the truth about what they see in you.

Who should you ask? Begin by identifying someone you trust and respect. You know this person won't massage the truth or lie just to make you feel better. Nor will they run you down. This person should also be someone who has nothing to gain by appeasing you and nothing to lose by offending you. You're not looking for a yes person. You're looking for a wholeness person. Actually, you're looking for a wholeness team, because you need more than one person who can speak truth into your life. Here's the principle to remember: "Wounds from a sincere friend are better than many kisses from an enemy" (Prov. 27:6 NLT). Empower your friends by giving them permission to be brutally honest with you about what they see. If they say something you don't want to hear, don't resist it. That's what they are there for. They are giving you a gift. If you could see the hard and the ugly on your own, you wouldn't need them. Consider what they say, and take it all in. It may sting for a moment, but it will create a lifetime of progress—and keep the thief of brokenness behind bars.

———————

These are the basic initial steps to help you recognize your broken areas. But it's not a once-and-for-all process. If you want to pursue wholeness, you need to be working these steps all the time. None of us gets a lifetime pass on pride and blind spots. Once you discover where you are broken, keep the process going. Every step you take will bring you closer to being made whole. As someone who has worked these steps for a while now, allow me to give you a heads-up. When the brokenness you didn't know you had is uncovered, you will likely have to battle off a mix of shame and pride. Shame—over your weakness or failures—will try to enlist pride as a covering. Remember how pride works? It wants you to deny it all, because if you can talk yourself out of being broken, there is nothing to feel any shame about. You can convince yourself that you were fine all along and go back to life as usual. But that would be a huge mistake and an obstacle on your path to wholeness. Don't be deceived. Don't take the pride bait. When shame and pride try to derail you, tell them you're not ashamed to be broken, and send them on their way. Embrace the rare gifts of humility and vulnerability, and let wholeness do what it does. And speaking of wholeness, let's talk about what happens once you recognize your brokenness.

SURRENDERING TO WHOLENESS

I'm not going to sugarcoat the truth. Once brokenness in your life is uncovered, you're going to feel naked, exposed, and vulnerable. That's definitely not a comfortable feeling. And chances are that you'll blush and scramble like Adam and Eve trying to find fig leaves to hide their privates. But let me say it again: there is no shame in any part of the process of getting whole. This is where the God of wholeness—the God who *is* Wholeness and who designed you to be whole—steps in and provides the covering of a beautiful healing process. Wholeness is drawn to our brokenness and covers us with love and affirmation. If Wholeness could sit right down next to you, I imagine you'd hear something like this:

In spite of your brokenness, I love you. In fact, I am the one who has orchestrated the uncovering. I don't expose you to shame you. I reveal your brokenness to you in order to heal you. I know what the completely whole version of you looks like, and I am always loving you into the person I created you to be.

I am the master potter, and to me you are valuable clay. I know exactly what you are supposed to look like in the end. So I put you on my wheel and I shape you and mold you. It is difficult for me to make you whole if you stiffen up or become brittle with pride. This keeps me from bringing out the beautiful details of your divine design. But if you will surrender, if you will relax like soft clay and trust my heart and my vision for you, I will fashion you into someone so beautiful that you will wish you had surrendered to me sooner.

Wholeness works only with humility and vulnerability. You can't be proud and whole at the same time. Wholeness loves truth and honesty. Wholeness doesn't see brokenness as a weakness, just a reality. In fact, the more willing you are to admit your brokenness, the closer you are to being made whole. You'll know something very powerful is happening in your life when you can boldly say, "I am broken!" So go ahead and say it now, out loud. Don't be afraid; just say it! Three words: "I am broken." There's nothing to be ashamed of. This is part of the process. The sooner you can say, "I am broken," the sooner you'll be able to say, "I am whole!"

Becoming whole takes work, but you are worth it. And you will never be alone in the process. Wholeness is with you in every step. Wholeness will guide you, affirm your value, and cover the process on your way to progress. Regardless of how broken your start may have been, Wholeness will see to it that your finish is breathtaking. There's more work to do, but because you've taken the time to walk through this process, you're already off to a great start on your journey. So let us continue on from brokenness to wholeness.

CHAPTER 5

THE CRACKED MIRROR

I'm not a big fan of amusement parks these days, but there was a time in my life when I lived for them. As a California kid, I loved going to Disneyland and Knott's Berry Farm every year. I especially enjoyed one particular attraction called the fun house. Remember the fun house, the one filled with all the crazy mirrors? Some mirrors distorted your image so you looked wide and bloated or tall and skinny. Others enlarged or shrunk the size of your head while keeping your torso the same size, creating an awkward cartoonlike figure. Still others made you look like a clown with huge feet or shrunk the space between your eyes so you looked like a Martian. These twisted images always made me and my friends laugh. I also found them fascinating because they weren't a total fabrication. Just distortions of our actual image that created a skewed perspective we found amusing.

In my efforts to help people find wholeness, I've observed a striking similarity between the fun house mirrors and brokenness. When a person is broken, their perceptions are skewed and distorted. They don't see things plainly. And it's no laughing matter when your life mirror is distorted or cracked. In fact, the only things you get out of that kind of crazy mirror are limitations, unhealthy expectations, and more brokenness.

In the previous chapter, we explored how brokenness operates and the harm it causes when it goes unacknowledged. Now we need to consider the residual effects that brokenness has in our lives, perhaps the most significant of which is a distorted perspective of both reality and ourselves. As we pursue wholeness, it's very important that we not neglect the issues lingering in the wake of our brokenness. It is possible to be healed and yet still need to mend the cracks and chasms that brokenness created in your life. We'll discuss this in more detail later in the book, but for now let's focus on the cracked and distorted mirrors that brokenness leaves us with.

YOUR INNER MIRROR

Each of us has what I call an inner mirror. The inner mirror helps us to interpret and understand what we see in our world, which then determines how we engage the people we relate to and the circumstances we live in. When that mirror is clear and healthy, it reflects accurate images of self, others, and the world around us, and those images enable us to respond in healthy and productive ways. However, when that mirror is distorted, we live with limitations and flawed expectations, which then attract and produce unhealthy outcomes.

When I was a little boy between five and seven years old, I routinely had nightmares about someone trying to harm me or my mother. I had great anxiety about something bad happening, and I never really felt safe. If it was just five minutes past my mother's normal time to arrive home from work, I began to panic. Things got so bad that my mother took me to see a psychologist. Although it was great to have a safe place to process my emotions, the fear itself never went away.

As I grew older, I had a very difficult time feeling safe no matter my environment. There were in fact real dangers in the inner-city neighborhood where we lived, but even when we later moved to a safer neighborhood in the suburbs, I still felt the need to be vigilant and cautious. Somehow, somewhere, as a little boy, I received a crack in the part of my inner mirror that reflected the safeness of my world. For years I tried to go back in time, looking for clues about what had distorted my inner mirror, and found nothing—until one day I remembered.

I was about five years old when my mom gave me a brand-new bike. I'll never forget it! It was shiny red and so much fun to ride. It was my first bike, and I loved the sense of freedom it gave me. I even had the courage to venture beyond our apartment parking lot and ride to the convenience store around the corner from our home to get a snack.

I pulled up to the store, laid down my bike just outside the entryway, and walked in. After buying a few sugary items, I walked back outside to get on my bike and ride home. I had been in the store for only a few minutes, but my bike was gone.

It was a surreal moment as I stood there trying to figure out how my bike could be there one moment and then be gone the next. I looked down the street in one direction and then in the other. There was no bike in sight. I was devastated. It felt like the greatest evil had just happened to me. Today I know better, but to my five-year-old self, things couldn't have been any worse. It was an experience that shook my young world, and I was traumatized.

That day something within me changed, and from that moment the world no longer felt safe. Instead it felt colder and darker. Even though I knew the incident happened during the day, oddly in my memory I recall it as happening at night. It *had* become nighttime for me, and the carefree, sunny days of my childhood were gone. This was the stone that cracked my inner mirror of safety, and it distorted my perspective of the world. It took decades and cost me years of peace before I could identify what had distorted my worldview on safety.

Your inner mirror determines how you perceive your world, yourself, others, and your circumstances. But it's important to note that a single incident may not distort how you see everything. For example, having my bike stolen didn't change the way I perceived myself. It didn't even necessarily change the way I saw others. What that crack in my mirror affected most was how I saw the world around me. Life itself was no longer safe, and I carried that perspective with me until I experienced wholeness and was healed from that brokenness and fear.

Perhaps you need to search your history for experiences

that may be at the root of your fears. For me it was a stolen bike; for you it could be something different that caused you to feel unsafe. There is a stone for every crack in your mirror, and pursuing wholeness requires that you find it.

A CRACKED WORLDVIEW

There are two common experiences that will almost always skew the way you see life. One of those, as in my case, is an unexpected loss. Prior to the theft of my bike, I was innocent; I had no reference point for loss. The world I lived in was safe and free from threat of harm. Little Touré didn't think twice about leaving his bike unlocked and unattended. But the unexpected loss of my bike stole my innocence; it cracked the image I had of the world as a safe and healthy place. You might be thinking that I was naive and that the world, in fact, is not a safe and healthy place. I have two responses to that. The first is that maybe your mirror is cracked too. (I bet you weren't expecting that.) It's funny but could also be true. The second thought is that although there are dangers in the world, there are also safe and healthy places here. In spite of the evil that exists, great things are happening all the time. The problem with having a distorted mirror is that a marred and negative worldview keeps us from seeing the peace, joy, and freedom that is available to us.

Disappointment is another experience that distorts our perspective on the world. Have you ever been let down,

I mean in a big way? You interviewed for the job, moved up through the hiring process, nailed the final interview, and prayed to get it, only to learn they hired someone else. You studied for a major exam, pulling all-nighters and giving it your best effort, yet still ended up with a poor grade. You had a dream-come-true relationship—the kind you thought would last forever—only to watch it crash and burn, leaving you in a daze, wondering what in the world just happened. There are so many things in life that disappoint us, from the loss of a loved one to life taking an unforeseen turn. Nothing robs us of an optimistic worldview quite like disappointment. Disappointments are crushing experiences, and they rarely leave us unscathed.

When losses and disappointments happen to you, if you don't process them properly, it creates a distortion on your inner mirror that changes both the way you see life and what you expect from life. This type of brokenness brings in an element of fear—fear that the same thing, or worse, might happen again. Fear then holds you hostage. When you're afraid of the unknown, you don't have the courage you need to take the legitimate and necessary risks required to grow and achieve. This is a debilitating brokenness that limits what is possible for you because it blinds you to all the good available in each moment. Then things get worse because once you expect negative outcomes, you begin to attract them. Your negative expectations create a subconscious sabotaging effect. Now you are no longer drawn to good things, because you are obsessed with bad ones. Even if a good thing presents itself, your cracked mirror keeps you from seeing it. Your distorted perspective skews the reality of good into something that will inevitably turn bad. And when you allow your disappointment to shape your expectations, you end up being disappointed over and over again. It's a terrible cycle. One I know well.

Little Touré's unsafe worldview later became teenaged Touré's fear of a premature death. I remember very sobering remarks I made at the birthday party my family threw for me when I turned eighteen. I said I felt grateful and blessed to have made it this far. All these years later, the words "this far" nearly bring me to tears. How sad is it for any young person to feel like merely surviving to eighteen is something remarkable? And how much sadder still for a young person to be robbed of the belief that good things await them? Although I'd experienced some misfortune by that point, if I had tallied up all my circumstances, I would have realized that I had experienced far more reasons to be optimistic and hopeful about my life. But my cracked mirror wouldn't allow me to see life that way. The signs indicating I had a bright future were all around me, but it would take time before I could recognize them.

And yet even in that darkness there was always a tiny flicker of hope beneath the surface. In fact, I've found that people who have suffered a great deal—even the most cynical—often still have a faint ray of hope that things could be different for them. It might be a dream suppressed by fear, something they try to argue against inwardly or explain away based on past disappointments, yet it still peeks through. What these individuals don't realize is that the hope that continues to emerge in them is evidence that the God of wholeness is inviting them to a better reality.

The first ray of hope I saw appeared when I was twelve and was bussed out of the inner city to a private school in the suburbs. Many of the children there had grown up in environments that were free from the kind of losses and disappointments that had cracked my mirror. Although they likely had other fears and issues, these young people weren't worrying about dying early. They didn't live in fear of being murdered in gang crossfire. Even though their reality and view of the world was different from mine, the freedom I witnessed in them began to rub off on me. I began to believe that maybe my life could be different after all.

Each day I got on the bus in one reality and was dropped off at school in a completely different reality. The bus didn't come all the way into my neighborhood but stopped just outside it. From there, we took a twenty-five-mile journey through neighborhoods that gradually improved until we reached our destination. Today I see that bus ride as a metaphor that demonstrates something about how experiencing wholeness heals a cracked and distorted inner mirror. Let me explain.

The experience of wholeness is the equivalent of the bus ride that carries us from one reality to another. It takes us from the reality of fear, past hurts, pessimism, and limitations to the reality of safety, peace, optimism, and infinite possibility. But before you can even get on the bus, you have to be willing to find and follow that faint ray of hope within you. You have to believe that your life can be different. You have to believe that the ray of hope within is the voice of Wholeness, and if you follow, he will lead you into a new and better life. Hope is what gets you out of your neighborhood of limitations and to the bus stop. That's the first step.

Then Wholeness pulls up to pick you up. That's right—not only is Wholeness the ray of hope that guided you to the bus stop, but Wholeness is also the bus. As you ride on the bus of Wholeness, you begin to notice how your environment is gradually changing. It doesn't happen all at once. But little by little, step by step, you begin to feel safer, more peaceful, and soon you arrive in the state of optimism, where you begin to believe that all things are possible. Wholeness is the voice, Wholeness is the vehicle, Wholeness is the journey, and Wholeness will be your destination.

Once I got on the bus, I began to see life more clearly. Wholeness helped me to understand that, yes, there is evil in the world, but there is much more goodness, and that goodness had been protecting me my entire life. He explained that I had focused only on the things that went wrong, not on the far more numerous things that went right every single day. Wholeness taught me that things would not always go as planned in this life, but not to fret; with him I could overcome even the worst of circumstances. Wholeness taught me that sometimes the miracle is not in being free from a difficult time but in being sustained through that difficult time. Wholeness taught me a lot on that bus, and I still enjoy riding it today.

After I had been on the bus for years, the bondage caused from my fear of dying young was healed. That healing freed me to expect and embrace all that Wholeness had lined up in my path. Maybe you see the world as I once did, or perhaps you feel stagnated by past hurts or disappointments. If you know your view of life is distorted and you want to find the courage and hope to dream again, the good news is that you can. The next step is learning how to recognize and take control of the narratives in your life.

EMBRACING THE NARRATIVE OF A HEALTHY SELF-IMAGE

There is almost always a correlation between the specific circumstances that caused our brokenness and the damage it did to our inner mirror. An individual who experiences a devaluing circumstance—verbal abuse, rejection, abandonment—will likely struggle with a poor self-image. If there is a crack in your mirror of self-perception, something in your past or present has created the crack. If you want to be whole—to develop and maintain a healthy image of self—you need to understand how to cultivate that healthy image. And nurturing that kind of new self-perception begins with the stories you tell yourself.

We all have what I like to call a storyteller. Your storyteller is the inner mechanism that tells you what is right or wrong about you. What your storyteller communicates, you almost automatically believe. Your storyteller tells you who you are, defines your value, and determines what you can or cannot do. There are many factors that shape the voice and tone of your storyteller. Your storyteller has a personality, and that personality is usually a hodgepodge of authoritarian voices you've encountered throughout your lifetime. Your storyteller might sound like your parents or your teachers, your sports coach or a religious leader, your boss or a trusted friend. Regardless of whose voice your storyteller mimics, it regulates your perceptions, and your perceptions are what become your reality. In life, you aren't who you are; you are who you *think* you are. For this reason, we must not only be aware of how our self-narrative shapes our reality but also be diligent to ensure that our self-narrative is being shaped by Wholeness rather than brokenness.

Cultivating a healthy self-image is about taking control of the narrative of your life and being diligent to question who the voice of your storyteller is at any given moment. Is my storyteller affirming me in my abilities or casting doubt and disbelief about what I am trying to accomplish? Is the voice of my storyteller encouraging me and cheering me on in life, or is it degrading me and causing me to always second-guess myself? Does my storyteller magnify everything it believes is wrong with me, or does it assure me of my competence, value, and worth? You cannot trust your storyteller—rely on your self-perceptions—until you are sure who the real narrator is. Wouldn't it be a shame if the voice that drives your self-image today is actually the voice of someone or something that wounded you yesterday? Sadly, I know exactly what that's like.

There was a time in my life when I wouldn't have even dreamed of allowing anyone outside of my family to throw me a party. Although I was popular throughout my school and college years and had scores of friends and associates, the idea of being celebrated by my friends was unthinkable to me. It wasn't that I was particularly modest or shy. The root issue was that I was afraid no one would show up. What's fascinating when I think about it today is that even if only a fraction of my friends had come, it still would have been a well-attended party. But there was something wrong with my storyteller. My storyteller said, "Nobody cares about you enough to show up at a party. You'll be sitting there by yourself. Save yourself the humiliation. No parties allowed." I wish I could tell you that I detected the crack in my mirror, fixed it, and threw myself a wild party to prove my storyteller wrong. But that's not what happened. However, what actually occurred became the catalyst for my healing. Several friends threw me a surprise party that was a massive hit and that we would talk about for years.

Why was my storyteller so afraid of the idea of having a party? I eventually traced my fear back to something that happened to me when I was nine years old. My mother and I had just moved to the Los Angeles area from Northern California, and I had to enroll in a new school. It was September, the beginning of the school year, and I had not yet made any friends. I was also experiencing a slight case of culture shock because my new inner-city surroundings were much different than what I was used to. In an attempt to help me make friends, my mother decided to throw me a birthday party. I didn't know who was or wasn't invited, but what I remember very vividly is that no one—I mean nobody—showed up. As you can imagine, I was devastated. Come on, *nobody*? That was a situation and a memory I wanted to quickly put behind me, so I buried it. Can you imagine how failing to process such an experience would affect a nine-year-old's psyche? What I couldn't have known at the time was that this buried memory would be resurrected in the narrative of my storyteller.

What I told myself at the time shaped my self-perception for many years to come: "There is something wrong with me. I'm not worth celebrating. My life hardly matters to anyone." What devastating thoughts to have in my formative years! The result? Decades later, a grown man's self-perception and self-narrative were still being shaped by the wounds and disappointments of a nine-year-old boy who had yet to experience wholeness.

As I've pursued wholeness, I've learned how to examine and qualify all of my apprehensions in life. In that healing process, I realized that my fear of being celebrated by friends was not only unhealthy but unfounded. In fact, I would later find out that through some logistic mishap, the invitations to my childhood party were never sent. The truth was that no one was ever invited, but the narrative of my brokenness convinced me that no one thought I mattered.

Just as good journalism requires fact-checking and verifying the source of information before publishing a story, developing and maintaining a healthy self-image requires verifying the source of your inner storyteller. Your life is far too valuable, and your potential far too great, to allow it to be shaped by any narrator but Wholeness. Wholeness has a perspective about who you are, what you can overcome, and who you will become. When the voice of Wholeness shapes your narrative, your self-perceptions will be uplifting and inspiring. This doesn't mean that Wholeness won't correct you when you're living outside your purpose and potential; Wholeness loves you too much to let you fall short of those. But with every correction, there will always be an arrow pointing up and a hand to lift you up.

Wholeness brings healthy perspectives to situations in your life that once brought you pain. Remember, unprocessed pain will always be ill-processed pain. Until you invite Wholeness into your painful areas to unmask the lies and guide you to the truth, you will default to the wrong storyteller, to wrong self-perceptions, to a wrong view of reality. And all of these wrongs have consequences, not only for your own life but also for your relationships.

CHARGING PEOPLE TODAY FOR THE SINS OF OTHERS YESTERDAY

How we see others is often a reflection of how we see ourselves. However, our perceptions of others can also be a reflection of our experiences with previous others. An inner mirror cracked by a painful experience with people in our past can greatly distort how we see others today. Just as it's important to have a healthy self-image, it's also important to have a healthy perspective on other people. Why? Because healthy relationships are a vital part of a healthy life. You can't ascend your mountain of potential while dragging the weight of damaged relationships behind you. You also can't achieve your potential alone. To become whole—to mature and become the highest version of yourself—you need to see and relate to others without distortions.

Is it possible that you might be charging someone in your life today for the sins of someone else from yesterday? Is there a chance that you are falsely accusing an innocent person of a crime someone else committed? If your inner mirror has been cracked by someone from the past, I can assure you that the answers to these questions are yes and yes. And it can happen with small cracks just as easily as it can with big ones. That's something I know from personal experience.

Once when my wife and children and I moved into a new home, we decided to continue using the landscaper the former owners had used for years. A few months after we moved, I noticed that one of the windows facing the back yard was cracked. I was puzzled about how that could have happened, so I decided to take a look at our security cameras to see if I could find out. To my surprise, it turned out to be one of the gardeners. He had been working with a weed-whacker that caught a pebble and threw it into the window. It was a harmless mistake and one that would have been easily forgivable, but there was a problem. The gardener made no mention of what happened. I was livid. I wasn't upset about a window cracked by accident. I could handle that. I was upset about the gardener's lack of integrity. Needless to say, I chose another landscaper to take care of our lawn.

For several months, I was very pleased with the new landscaper. His work was excellent, and he was fair and honest. But then one morning I received his invoice and was about to write a check when I noticed that the total was higher than it should have been. One of the line items was from a previous invoice that had already been paid. I immediately began to suspect that this was not a simple mistake, that this gardener also lacked integrity and was trying to take advantage of me. My inner narrator spun out an elaborate story of how he was surely double-charging me because he thought I was too busy to notice. Before long, I had a whole narrative going about how our new gardener was a part of a landscaping crime ring focused on overcharging unsuspecting suburban homeowners. Pretty ridiculous, right?

I was upset, but I also knew I had to do some fact-checking and verifying of sources, so I gave the gardener a call. It turned out to be a simple oversight. He had an unsophisticated accounting system and hadn't yet input my last payment. He wasn't a crook, he didn't lack integrity, and from what I could tell, he was not the leader of a landscaping crime ring. He was just an honest guy who made a mistake. I had charged him falsely. My cracked mirror—caused by the previous gardener's cracked window—skewed my perception of all landscapers, nearly costing me the best one I had ever worked with.

I've come up with a strategy I believe can help us combat our tendency to judge others based on past experiences. If we get this discipline down and allow it to be our new normal, we will be less likely to charge someone falsely. I call this strategic discipline "thinking the highest thought."

Thinking the highest thought is making a conscious decision to believe the best about an individual when you do not have hard evidence to prove otherwise. It's giving others the benefit of the doubt. Now, I realize that putting this discipline into practice may be a struggle, especially if your inner mirror has lots of cracks. There is a risk in always aiming to think the highest thought about others. What if you think the highest thought and you're wrong? What might being wrong cost you? Although those are valid concerns, you also have to consider the flip side. What if you think the lowest thought and you're wrong? What might being wrong cost you then? I'd rather think the highest thought about a person and be wrong than think the lowest thought and condemn someone who doesn't deserve it.

Thinking the highest thought doesn't mean that you entrust or empower people whose integrity is questionable. That's not at all what I'm saying. You should never blindly disregard your discretion. Mitigating risks is being responsible. What I am saying is that it will always be better—for you and for others—to believe the best of people than to believe the worst of them. Another way to think about this is to consider what it's like to be on the receiving end of someone else's lowest thoughts.

In my role as a pastor, I've often experienced being charged with the sins of others. I've noticed this pattern especially among some of the youngsters who feel upset and hurt when my schedule won't allow a timely sit down with them. I am by no means rejecting them, but with a congregation several thousand members large, it is impossible for me to meet personally with everyone who desires to meet, so I've empowered other staff members to help. Most people understand, but I observe that some of our younger congregants seem to take my inability to meet with them personally. They become upset, and I can sense that they feel rejected. As I've taken a closer look, I've found out that many of these young people are charging me with the sins of their parents, those who weren't present enough. In many instances, their parents have committed themselves to work, seeking to create a better life for them. The tradeoff is that this approach keeps the parents from creating a good life *with* them. For these young people in our church, I represent much more than a spiritual leader; I've become their surrogate father. And when I too appear to be too busy to make time for them, I catch the blame for the sins of their parents.

This is a complicated and painful reality for all involved. It never feels good to be rejected, and it never feels good to have your actions misunderstood. I truly love every member of our church and the hard work that keeps me so busy is motivated by that love for them and the desire to see each one flourish. What they perceive as rejection because of their cracked mirror is really my commitment to doing all I can to help them the best way I know how. In this and in many other instances, thinking the highest thought will make a world of difference. Imagine if the young congregant refused to accept the narrative that my busyness or that of their parents is rejection but instead searched for other evidence that proved our concern and care. What if they said to themselves, "Maybe their busyness is actually proof of their love for me, because what they are busy doing will somehow add value to me in other ways." Sure, there will always be times to communicate our need for more quality time, but let's not assume the lack of it equates to a lack of love or value. Wholeness allows you to be optimistic about all things and gives you the grace to reimagine what could otherwise be painful.

TRUSTING AGAIN

At the end of the day, healing your cracked inner mirror comes down to trusting again. Wholeness wants to give you confidence in the good that exists out there. In fact, as you learn to listen to the voice of Wholeness, you'll begin to have new perspectives. The cracks on your mirror will begin to clear, and you will begin to see the sunny days of restoration on the horizon. Wholeness will keep you from sabotaging your future, by instructing you on how not to charge your present with the crimes from your past. Remember, when the voice of brokenness controls your inner narrative, the stories you tell yourself—about life, self, and others—will exaggerate and reinforce the insecurities, fears, and pains of the past. When the voice of Wholeness controls your inner narrative, the stories you tell yourself will often challenge, or provide a different perspective on, the circumstances that caused you pain.

Wholeness is a healer and knows how to take the hurt that caused our brokenness and turn it into strength. The voice of Wholeness will always be affirming, encouraging, and empowering. Wholeness will give you healthy expectations and the fortitude to reel in the blessings that disappointment and self-protection try to throw back. Even though it's hard sometimes, you do have a choice: You can think the highest thought. You can believe the best things. And when you encounter a setback, don't fret. Setbacks are a routine part of life and growth. Wholeness will see you through those times too. It may not always happen the way you expect or as quickly as you hope, but pursuing your own wholeness will always give you victory. Wholeness is calling you. All he needs is your vulnerability, your trust, and your hunger for change. If you offer these things regularly, Wholeness will do the rest.

CHAPTER 6

INNER SECURITY

One of the main things that drives the work I do is my belief in the potential of every person I encounter, and my confidence in who they can become. That's my passion—helping people tap into the greatness I see when I look at them. In fact, I'm so convinced about who people can become and what they can achieve that I often find myself in the mind-boggling position of being more confident about them than they are about themselves! Several years ago, I even had a dream about it.

I dreamed I was on a distant planet with my firstborn daughter, Ren. We were standing in a lush and beautiful countryside that was surrounded by mountains, green pastures, and peaceful bodies of water. However, all was not well. On the horizon, we could see hordes of threatening and wicked inhabitants swiftly approaching. There was seemingly no way for us to escape. Fearing for my daughter's life, I began to passionately admonish her, "Fly, baby, fly!"

Ren looked at me with a mix of fright and confusion. "I can't fly, Daddy," she cried. "I can't!"

"Yes, you can, baby," I implored. "Yes, you can—just stretch out your arms!"

Although she stretched out her arms a little, she still cried out, "I can't, Daddy. I can't!" Meanwhile, the evil throngs were drawing nearer. The closer they got, the more impassioned my pleas and hurried my instructions.

"Fly, baby, fly. You can do it!"

"I can't, Daddy. I can't!"

"Just start moving your arms!"

As our situation grew increasingly desperate, something began to change in Ren. Although she was still frightened, she finally allowed herself to believe me, and she started to ascend. Just as we were about to be overcome, Ren's gift of flight carried us away from certain death to safety.

In the dream, I saw something in my daughter she couldn't see in herself. My love for her drove me to challenge her, to help her rise above what she thought were her limitations. With affirmation and encouragement, I urged her to take a risk, to become the person I knew she had the potential to be. I challenged her insecurities and empowered her to soar.

The dream was about my daughter and me, but I believe it also reveals something true about every person who will ever live on this planet. Those threatening hordes on the horizon? They represent the plethora of fears and insecurities many of us face every day. However, too often we are so locked into our feelings of helplessness and limitations that we succumb to them rather than rise above them. But as we learn more about our insecurities—where they come from and how to overcome them—we can begin to soar above them. To do so, we have to be willing to listen to the voice of Wholeness. Wholeness loves us relentlessly and sees us not according to the way we see ourselves but according to who and what he knows we can become. Wholeness knows we can rise above our limitations and even now is challenging us, empowering us to "Fly, baby, fly!"

INSECURITY

To rise above insecurity, you need to understand exactly what it is. Insecurity is the absence of inner security. It is the result of not feeling safe, covered, protected, or confident. Remember, as we discussed in chapter 3, your inner person is the most delicate and sensitive part of yourself. It's who you are underneath, the part of you that needs to be loved, affirmed, accepted, and valued. The mere thought of being rejected or devalued is frightening to your inner self, and that fear is what creates insecurity.

I've seen this dynamic play out over and over again at our church. Some careers even exacerbate insecurity. For example, we have a lot of actors in our congregation, and one of the things I've learned from them over the years is that being an undiscovered actor can be brutal on a person's sense of security. Especially the audition process. Getting a job requires going to as many auditions as possible and hoping for a callback, which will then lead to either booking the job or another round of auditions, called a "test," to determine which candidate ultimately gets the job. All this requires long drives to audition locations and long hours in tiny waiting rooms where actors sit (or stand) awkwardly among their competitors, all waiting their turn to be called into "the room." But the most difficult part is what happens once an actor finally makes it into the room.

There are bright lights that illuminate every imperfection the actor has tried to camouflage, and a camera with an intimidatingly large lens. The actor must now "slate," stating and spelling out his or her name. The audition has begun, and everything about the actor is being studied and scrutinized for acceptance or rejection. But there's no feedback, and often actors won't have any indication of how they did unless they get the coveted callback. Once the audition is complete, the actor is quickly dismissed and the next candidate is called in. Part of an actor's job description is essentially to be repeatedly rejected in the hope that they might one day be accepted, only to go right back into the rejection cycle, looking for their next big break once that job is complete.

What makes this cycle even more brutal is that the rejection is personal. Unlike rejection faced in other lines of work, such as car sales or telemarketing, there is no separation between the product and the person, between what actors are offering and who they are. When actors are turned down for a job, who they are is rejected, and only few are whole enough to emerge from repeated rejections without insecurities. For this reason and others, I advise the actors who join our church to make sure they are pursuing wholeness before they even think about going to an audition.

You and I may not have "repeated rejection" on our job descriptions, but we all end up auditioning in one way or another. Sometimes we spend great amounts of time in the mirror before leaving the house because we are auditioning for the approval of our fellow students or coworkers. Other times we present only the best news at family gatherings because we are auditioning for the approval of our relatives. We all have a great need for approval and acceptance. If we haven't experienced wholeness, that need can become a gaping hole in our inner person, creating debilitating insecurities and locking us into an endless cycle of auditions and rejections.

WHOLENESS HEALS INSECURITY

When we experience wholeness, we exchange our insecurities for what I call inner security. Inner security is a state of unshakeable confidence that comes from the foundational knowledge that we are truly loved by God. It is composed of an absolute, unconditional, irreversible love that affirms us, celebrates us, and accepts us at all times. The God of wholeness not only bestows this rare type of love upon us but is himself that love. The love of Wholeness is hard to grasp, because it is vastly different from every other type of love in the human experience. It's in a league of its own. Most types of love we experience are based on mutual affinities, similar interests, relational proximity, or commonality. We love our family, our friends, and people who are kind to us.

This means that most of the love we have come to experience is based on some degree of reciprocity. The love we receive from Wholeness is different in that it is love with no strings attached. It's not responsive love; it's immutable love, and that's why you can trust it. It's love that gave, love that gives, and love that will never cease giving.

The real you needs that type of love. Your inner self is wired for it. A lesser love will always leave room for insecurities. When love in your life is conditional, there is no guarantee it will last forever. This threat of love leaving creates instability and insecurity. This type of insecurity causes people to make terrible decisions. I've seen people so desperate to hold on to relationships that they give away pieces of themselves in hopes of keeping their partner's love. Almost always their plan backfires and the partner leaves, taking away not only their so-called love but the pieces of the person they left. To be a secure and whole person, you need love that's better than that. You need love that covers and protects the most vulnerable part of yourself. When you feel that your inner self is protected, affirmed, and loved, a whole, secure, and confident version of yourself is produced.

UPROOTING AN INSECURITY

An insecurity is like a persistent weed that needs to be uprooted. So let's take a closer look at the four steps required to understand, confront, and eliminate it.

1. Discern the Feelings

If we were to poll a group of people and ask them what it means to be insecure, chances are we would get answers that describe feelings such as fear, inadequacy, vulnerability, self-doubt, lack of confidence, uncertainty, low self-esteem, self-hatred, and anxiety. It's important when uprooting an insecurity that you first take time to identify precisely what you feel. For example, you may feel unqualified, not smart enough, or unattractive. Once you can identify the specific feelings that insecurity causes, you have the first clue that will lead you to the root of your insecurity problems.

2. Identify the Thought beneath the Feelings

Did you know that feelings are traceable to thoughts? Although insecure *feelings* are what we tend to notice first, every insecurity begins with a thought. In fact, an insecurity is actually evidence of a negative, untrue, and devaluing thought.

Underneath everything we feel is a thought or an idea that is making us feel that particular way. When we are confident and motivated, there is an underlying thought of optimism that we can achieve something. When we are discouraged, the underlying thought is that we lack something and are unsure if we can arrive at a positive outcome. Every feeling is traceable to a thought, an underlying belief about who we are. In fact, when you experience feelings of insecurity, think of it as an alert that is calling your attention to an unhealthy thought lurking somewhere in your mind.

"Regina" is a woman from our church who was struggling

with insecurity issues—specifically, a feeling of inadequacy because she never felt smart enough. During a counseling session, I asked if she could recall a time in her life when she did feel smart and confident. As she paused and thought for a few moments, she remembered a time as a little girl when she was confident, did well in school, and saw herself as bright and smart. Although she had entered my office looking overwhelmed and downcast, when she described this time in her life, she lit up and began to beam. Observing the change in her countenance, I sat back for a moment, allowing her to live in that positive reality for a while. She needed to remember what it was like to feel that way, so she could identify when that feeling of confidence and affirmation left her life.

After a few minutes, I asked her when she thought things changed, and what someone in her life may have said that caused her to question herself. I asked this very important question because usually insecurity doesn't happen without some involvement of others. Someone bruises our inner security, and that bruise becomes the entry point for our insecurity.

Regina gave it some thought and then recalled a particularly damaging episode from her childhood when her alcoholic and abusive father had ridiculed her. "He called me a dumb blonde," she said. As a child, Regina attached much of the abuse she'd experienced to this one comment. Her young mind reasoned that her father mistreated her because she wasn't smart enough to be worthy of his love. His words lodged a fiery arrow in her heart, initiating a downward spiral of rejection, inadequacy, and insecurity that continued for decades. It also launched her on a desperate search for affirmation wherever she could find it, which often meant selling herself short to gain the approval of others. Because one of the first and most important authority figures in her life had told her she was inadequate, Regina carried this thought within as a true statement about who she was. Fortunately, with some digging, we were able to get down to the root of her insecurity. It had all begun with a thought that was shaped by harsh treatment and harsh words from her father.

3. Name the Storyteller and Debunk the Lie

Determining whether a thought is true comes down to one question: Who said it? Who is the author of the story you are telling yourself? In life, it isn't what others say to you that matters the most; it's what you say to yourself that's critical. Unfortunately, we won't always be able to keep our ears from hearing the piercing words of others. That's a part of life. Hurt people hurt people, which is why the pursuit of wholeness never ends. Pursuing wholeness is what enables us to distinguish the self-defeating words spoken by brokenness from the life-giving words spoken by Wholeness.

Once Regina tracked down the thought beneath her feelings of insecurity, it was time to consider the source of the thought and to debunk it for the lie that it was. I wanted Regina to discover for herself that the thought that led to the insecurity was untrue. Then she would be able to admit to herself that her feelings of inadequacy were unfounded. As we talked, Regina began to understand that her inner mirror had been cracked by the words and behavior of her father. Now she could name the voice behind her insecurities; her storyteller was her own brokenness. She wept on behalf of the little girl who had lived so long with a broken mirror, but her tears were ones of healing and release as she finally let go of the lie. She made the decision that day to listen only to the voice of Wholeness, the storyteller who could heal her inner mirror and help her to grow in truth and love.

As you grow and become whole, you will become more familiar with and attuned to the voice of Wholeness. When your storyteller tears you down rather than affirming that you are uniquely and wonderfully created, you'll know it's not Wholeness speaking. Wholeness will always affirm your value and your worth. Any voice or thought that is demeaning, belittling, or discouraging is not Wholeness.

Now that she had named the storyteller and debunked the lie, the next step for Regina was to renovate her mind with the truth. What truth had Wholeness been saying to her all along that was drowned out by the lie brokenness had been telling her?

4. Renovate Your Mind

Even when you've debunked the lie, you will naturally default to the story you've been telling yourself for years. It's not enough to simply tell yourself that the story isn't true. To experience wholeness, you must renovate your mind with truth. How? By tearing down the old story and repeatedly telling yourself a new story that builds you up instead of tearing you down.

In any renovation, there is usually a demolition before there is a new construction. The old is knocked down and the new is raised up. In the process of overcoming insecurity, we take the jackhammer of truth to lies and false narratives, again and again. It's not a once-and-for-all operation but a steady and repeated process, one that continues until what's old is gone. We renovate our minds by taking the truths that Wholeness speaks and using them to demolish the old thoughts and lies.

In her pursuit of wholeness, Regina focused on the voice of Wholeness, which told her she was brilliant, valuable, exceptional, and wonderful. When feelings of insecurity tried to creep back in, she pulled out her jackhammer of truth. Her transformation from insecurity to wholeness didn't happen overnight, but it did happen. Over time, she began to naturally think new thoughts about herself. It took diligence, hard work, and intentionality, but Regina would be the first to tell you that it was more than worth the effort.

After hearing Regina's story, did any of your own weeds of insecurity come to mind? Has something ever been said to you that made you second-guess yourself? My counseling experience leads me to believe that your answer is most likely yes. If so, the good news is that you don't have to let those weeds sink deeper roots. By developing the habit and discipline of these four steps, you can uproot your insecurities and take your next steps to a much more confident and empowered version of you.

WHAT IF?

Have you ever wondered who you could become if you were free of insecurities? What might you accomplish if you could be secure within yourself no matter your environment? The lies beneath your insecurity want to dim your light, but Wholeness created you to shine. Allow yourself to dream a little, to imagine a new life, to ask, What if?

If you struggle with insecurity of any kind, make up your mind today that it will not be a part of your future. Regina's life changed for the better, and today she's living life with no limits. She already had wings; she just needed to hear and believe the voice urging her to "Fly, baby, fly!" I believe the voice of Wholeness is saying the same thing to you. It's time for you to let go of your self-imposed limitations, to let go of the lies, to believe the truth about who you really are. *Fly, baby, fly!* Stretch out your wings and soar on the truth. Let Wholeness lift you high above fear and insecurity, showing you life from a whole new vantage point.

Let's go! It's time to get whole.

CHAPTER 7

TWO HALVES DON'T MAKE A WHOLE

The journey to becoming whole is full of many good surprises but also includes some painful revelations, especially about things in our lives that our brokenness let in. The more whole you become, the more clearly you see the things that were relevant only to the broken version of you. And when the infrastructure of a life is built primarily by brokenness, the only cure is a complete renovation of that life from the inside out. I experienced this painful but healing process firsthand when I had to say goodbye to a long-term relationship, one I had built my very identity upon.

I met her when I was eighteen years old and a freshman in college. It was a time in my life when I believed that things were finally looking up. I was leaving behind an environment in which I rarely felt safe and escaping a cast of shady characters who only reinforced my distrust of people. The campus was in the suburbs, about forty-five miles outside the inner-city neighborhood where I'd grown up.

I was now an on-campus resident and no longer had to look over my shoulder, wondering if I would be the next victim of a shooting, robbery, or some other random act of violence. I wanted a quality education, but going to college was also about escape. My insecurities had me running away from the fears that began when I was a five-year-old and my bike was stolen. One day, my running took the form of walking into a student lounge, where I met the woman with whom I'd spend the next two decades of my life.

To be honest, my initial attraction to her was completely physical. She was a beautiful girl with a distinguishing shape, and I took notice. I'm not proud of the type of young man I was at the time. My view of young women up to that point had been formed by my experiences with a series of girls, some promiscuous, who had proven untrustworthy. I experienced my first heartbreak early in life and had convinced myself that no young woman could be trusted; I would never allow myself to be vulnerable again. Going forward, I was determined that any relationship would have to benefit me exclusively. My mirror had been cracked, and this caused me to indict every young woman I encountered for the crimes of the few, until I experienced wholeness and began to heal from the brokenness which created this behavior. Unfortunately, that healing didn't happen before I met her.

When I approached her, my intentions were not pure, and after a couple failed attempts at seducing her, I realized she was different from the other girls I had encountered. Her goodness intrigued me, and after getting to know her better,

I learned she had been sheltered from life as I knew it, in what looked like a stable family. In my eyes, she was innocent and pleasantly naive. Most important, she felt safe. In retrospect, I realize that she represented the exact opposite of all the fears I was trying to escape. Rather than falling in love with the person she was, I fell in love with the idea of her and the promise of safety that idea represented. She was a beautiful girl with a great heart, but that is not what captivated me. What my brokenness, fear, and insecurity needed more than anything was a safe existence, the promise of a bright future, and someone who could introduce me to a world I had never experienced. In truth, what I needed was wholeness, but I was ignorant to its availability, and so I clung to her instead. Together we set out on a tumultuous twenty-year journey of codependency, feeding the voids caused by each other's areas of brokenness but never truly becoming whole.

WHEN BROKENNESS BUILDS THE HOUSE

Anything that brokenness builds can be sustained only if brokenness ensues. Brokenness and Wholeness use entirely differently materials to build a life. Wholeness uses materials such as confidence, optimism, love, selflessness, generosity, and graciousness. Brokenness uses materials such as fear, insecurity, jealousy, manipulation, craftiness, selfishness, and control. When Wholeness enters a life, he shines a spotlight of truth on everything built by brokenness. Damaged walls and infrastructure that once appeared normal or went unnoticed are now exposed for what they really are—faulty construction.

Although the difficulties in our relationship began right away, it would take years and lots of counseling with a therapist before I could see things clearly. I remember sitting in my weekly counseling session one time, struggling to make sense of how our relationship had deteriorated. I couldn't understand why our marriage had ultimately broken down during what was otherwise the most awakened period of my life. Wholeness was healing me, leading me higher up the mountain of my potential. How could my life be being made whole in every area except my relationship with her? Why was it that the more wholeness I experienced, the less genuine our relationship seemed to become? Undeniably, we had experienced some great times together, and we produced three wonderful children along the way, yet there was little else between us.

I can still remember the moment when the lightbulb came on during a counseling session. When my therapist asked me a series of questions about the origins of our relationship, an obvious but previously unrecognized truth emerged. From the start, codependency, not love, was the foundation of our union. I fell silent, tears welled in my eyes, and a deep emptiness filled my chest. I felt broken by the truth. I also felt relieved that this realization came at the close of our session, which allowed me to dart to my car, shut the door, and cry privately. It felt like my therapist, a master surgeon, had reached right into my chest and pulled something out—a part of my infrastructure that had been built by brokenness.

From the beginning, my insecurities and fears had placed demands on the relationship that it could never fulfill. In fact, the relationship had become a critical component of my infrastructure, and I was relying on it to provide the safety, security, and assurance of goodness that only an experience with the God of wholeness can provide. I can recall times early on when our incompatibility was undeniable, but the risk of losing what had been my refuge made my fear of leaving greater than the pain of staying. When the therapist confronted my faulty building material that masqueraded as security, the void was exposed and I had to address the truth.

Wholeness has no sympathy for our attachments to things procured or built by brokenness, regardless of how long they've been in our lives. Wholeness knows the plans he has for us, and only the whole version of us will be able to get there. Wholeness trains his sights on anything in our lives that keeps us from becoming whole, so it can be transformed or released. In this instance, becoming whole required a complete letting go.

That day in the therapist's office was one of the hardest days of my life, but strangely, it was also one of the most liberating. As difficult a truth as it was to hear, it was a truth that had come to set me free. When the dust settled, we were both made whole, although as individuals rather than a couple. The God of wholeness has a way of ensuring that all things will ultimately work together for good. He redeems our most painful experiences and sets us back on the path to fulfill his larger and more glorious plan.

FIVE MUST-HAVES BEFORE SAYING "I DO"

My own journey from a painful divorce to a now thriving marriage afforded me valuable insights about relationships that not only have helped me personally but also have enabled me to offer hope and guidance to millions of people around the world. Who you choose to spend your life with is one of the most important decisions you can ever make. Relationships are vital and if chosen and managed well can become the most meaningful, fulfilling, and rewarding experiences of your life. Relationships can make you or break you, which means that choosing well is critical. Over the years, I've narrowed down my list of insights to five things every couple must have before taking their relationship to the next level. If any of these five are lacking, put your relationship on hold immediately and don't even think about marrying anytime soon. I realize that this may seem harsh or perhaps abrupt, but it is very important. This doesn't mean that your relationship isn't going to work if these are missing. It does mean, however, that there are significant enough concerns that should motivate you to slow down long enough to get the counseling you need before moving things forward. Here are the five things that should be in place.

1. Chemistry

A relationship grounded in wholeness has chemistry. By chemistry, I don't mean sexual arousal or misty-eyed romanticism. I mean a mutual attraction that creates a new kind of energy in you and between you. When two souls have chemistry, an intangible something within is awakened. You've likely heard the saying "It was love at first sight." Although I am skeptical about the phrase and encourage due diligence in qualifying "love," I do believe that chemistry is spontaneous, automatic, and happens instantaneously. Chemistry doesn't always present itself as romantic love; often it shows up as a peaceful familiarity. It's an acknowledgment that something beyond the two of you is also happening between the two of you.

So what does chemistry look like in practical terms? Perhaps the best way to describe it is to share what it was like when I first met Sarah, my wife. Although we met in the context of a business meeting that included others, I felt especially drawn to her. As we sat in each other's presence and talked back and forth, it was apparent that something beyond us was happening between us. Sarah is a beautiful woman, but what stood out most to me in that initial meeting was how beautiful she was on the inside. I was captivated by everything she said. I had never encountered another human soul who could articulate the complexities of life in a way that so resonated with my own perspectives and experience. I sometimes even marveled that I wasn't the one speaking! It was surreal. However, that's as far as things went at that point.

Although I was touched by the encounter, I had no desire to date Sarah, nor did I perceive her in any romantic way. It was a pure experience of chemistry, and I walked away from that meeting thinking that this particular young woman was very special. We agreed to do business in the future, but we each went back to life as usual.

There is a reason why chemistry is merely the first component in a relationship: it still has to be tested and qualified. We need to discern whether it's true chemistry or a lesser chemistry based only on something like physical attraction or shared interests. The fact is, you can experience a lesser form of chemistry multiple times, even in one day. One of the saddest things I often witness is when two people fall in love at a chemistry level. Inevitably, the relationship ends as quickly as it began, because chemistry was never designed to sustain a relationship. Chemistry characterized by wholeness is pure, but it is still just the starting point for a lifelong relationship.

2. Connection

Connection is chemistry all grown up. It's when that intangible something that was awakened within you at the chemistry stage begins to become love. I remember the precise moment I experienced connection with Sarah.

Our paths crossed again one month after our first meeting. We were both attending a large conference in Orlando hosted by Sarah's father, and somehow we managed to run into each other in a crowd of thousands. We noticed and greeted each other but headed our separate ways to attend the first session of the day. Then the texting began. We sent each other notes about the message being taught and how it resonated so much with the conversation we'd had in our first meeting. After the session ended, we went our separate ways once more until we ran into each other again at the evening session.

In an auditorium filled with thousands of people, Sarah and I somehow ended up sitting right beside each other in the front row. I sensed that something bigger than us was happening. Again we enjoyed the message and sharing notes. At the end of the session, Sarah's father, who was facilitating, stood on the platform and asked each person to take the hand of their neighbor as he prepared to close the session in prayer. When I stretched out my hand to take hers, it felt like our hands came together perfectly. It was as if her hands were made for mine, and mine for hers. There was a comfort and familiarity that spoke to us clearly, saying this moment was supposed to be.

After I fought through a jumble of nerves (I was, after all, standing in front of Bishop Jakes and holding his youngest daughter's hand), I was able to concentrate on the riveting things happening inside me. I realized in the core of my being that I was not holding the hand of a stranger. I knew that Sarah meant something to my life—something deep and special—but I didn't know exactly what it was, because I had never felt it before. What I was feeling was connection, and from that moment forward I longed to see her again. Connection is the second component of a whole relationship, but even connection has to be tested.

3. Wholeness

You might think that if you can check off both chemistry and connection, then chances are you've found your destiny mate. Not so fast. I pride myself on being inspirational, and I don't enjoy bursting anyone's bubble, but let me be clear: there are many things that can cause two people to feel "connected." Sometimes that connection is rooted in brokenness. I know all too well the deception of brokenness. Codependency does a stellar job masquerading as love. I've experienced it in my own life and have counseled countless people who have been seduced by their own brokenness and called it love. The only way you can know if your connection is true love is to first become whole so you can learn to tell the difference.

In this life, we will always be a work in progress, but we can also experience increasing levels of wholeness from which we can make sound decisions. Whole people make whole decisions. Broken people make broken decisions that end up creating even more brokenness. There is a proverb that brilliantly illustrates this: "To the hungry soul every bitter thing is sweet" (Prov. 27:7 KJV). If you're starved, you'll eat anything. When we are broken, our inner person is starved, needy, and sometimes desperate. Anything that appears to feed our need becomes irresistible, even if it's bitter, even if it can ultimately destroy us. Therefore before we fully commit to a connection, we need to test it and qualify it to make sure it isn't brokenness masquerading as love.

A couple weeks after seeing each other in Orlando, Sarah and I decided to meet in Los Angeles for dinner. During our dinner date, it truly felt like time stood still as we shared our hearts with one another. As it turned out, we talked for three hours and only stopped then because the restaurant was closing. That evening, our connection grew even deeper as we shared many life experiences, what we had come to understand about life, and the greatest lessons we'd learned. That was the night that Sarah and I suspected for the very first time that we had found love.

I dropped her off at her lodging place, hugged her courteously, and wished her a good evening. I remember driving home that night feeling like I was living on a completely different planet. I couldn't wrap my head around what had just happened to me, and so quickly. I was overwhelmed by the love I felt for Sarah, but at the same time I began to feel anxious. *What if this isn't love?* I thought. *What if this is just infatuation?* My heart had deceived me in the past. What if this was just another trick?

For a period of time before meeting Sarah, I had decided that I would not date anyone. I took that time to pursue my own wholeness and to grow spiritually, and I didn't want to be distracted from that process. *Is Sarah a distraction?* Prior to meeting her, I had finally come to a place where I was content with myself—by myself. I had become whole enough to not need anyone else in order to feel safe and complete. I was in a great place, and now this. *Is my brokenness trying to lead me astray once again?*

With all these questions circulating in my head, there was only one thing to do: let Sarah go. And that's exactly what I did. I went home and decided that I was taking back my heart.

I told myself there was a possibility that this "love" wasn't real, and the only way to find out was to let it go completely. That was it. I surrendered our relationship with no expectation for its return. I went to bed with total peace because I knew I had been healed from the brokenness that once made me needy. I was happily single before I met Sarah, and I could be happy by myself again. The end. Or at least that's what I thought.

In the early hours of the next morning, during my usual time of prayer and spiritual reading, I don't know how else to say it except that the truth was made plain. I felt confirmed that not only was it real love that Sarah and I felt for each other but Sarah was indeed to be my wife. As crazy as it sounds, I recognized in the entirety of my being that this was true. Letting go of Sarah was a kind of test to see if I really was whole, and I passed! It also helped me to understand what the process of making a whole decision looks and feels like.

The God of wholeness has no desire to keep anything from you. In fact, God has ordained the very best things for you in life. His plans are to prosper you and never to harm you. But to get you there, your brokenness has to be healed. When that happens, you are no longer blindly driven by your hungry soul. Instead you can accurately discern the bitter things from the sweet things, the broken things from the whole things. The God of wholeness had a sweet thing named Sarah in store for me, and to this very day I'm amazed by the gift she is to my life.

What I didn't know was that prior to meeting me, Sarah had made the same decision not to date and to work on being whole. The God of wholeness had been working behind the scenes for our good all along. When I called Sarah and told her about the confirmation I'd received, she with both excitement and sobriety agreed, and we were married just eight months later. As we once again stood in front of her father holding hands, we exchanged our vows against the backdrop of a gorgeous sunset and couldn't help but recall that first connection moment in Orlando. Our hand-holding moment then had foreshadowed what was to come—this very moment we were standing in, now as husband and wife.

Be brave enough to qualify your connection through the test of wholeness. By doing so, you have nothing but brokenness to lose, and all the blessings of a whole relationship to gain.

4. Divine Confirmation

The fourth must-have component before you can commit to marriage is divine confirmation. There need to be things beyond you, assuring you that this relationship is being orchestrated and blessed by the God of wholeness. I'm not talking about hyperspiritual validations that any desperate mind seeking a certain answer can drum up. The God who wants you to be whole needs none of that to prove that he is at work in your life. The kind of divine confirmations I'm talking about will come without you even looking for them. That's the beauty of it. These are not signs that are within your control. They are little graces along the way that whisper or joyfully proclaim that this is the person for you.

These signs are very important because brokenness will always attempt to sabotage the real thing either before or after you commit to marriage. Remember, just because you reach a level of wholeness in one area doesn't mean you are free from brokenness in others. Brokenness is relentless. Consequently, it is important that you know from the onset that the two of you didn't bring yourselves together; the God of wholeness did. That way, when trouble comes to test the strength of your relationship, you'll know in the heat of the battle that you're destined to overcome it. Any relationship God initiates, God provides unlimited power to maintain. If you hang in there and stay in the fight, victory is inevitable. It might take some effort, some soul-searching, and sometimes a great deal of work, but you'll know that it's worth it because the God of wholeness never leads us wrong.

Divine confirmations can come in a variety of forms, but you'll recognize them when they arrive. They are heaven-sent postcards and love notes encouraging you to stay the course because the God of wholeness is with you.

For Sarah and me, there were too many to recount, although one that stands out involved our books. While we were dating, we both published new books. The books were on unrelated topics, yet readers and even the major book retailers regularly displayed them together. Dozens of social media posts included our book covers—with our faces on them—side by side, with captions that praised their content. This happened months before we made our relationship public. You could call it a coincidence, or you could call it a divine love note, a confirmation that the God of wholeness had been orchestrating our union long before we came together.

That's how powerful divinely ordained relationships are, and if the relationship is truly orchestrated by God, authentic and powerful confirmations will be plenteous.

5. A Sense of Purpose

The last thing on my shortlist of must-haves in qualifying a destiny companion is a sense of purpose. Romance is a wonderful thing, and having a best friend to spend your life with is a blessing, but when the God of wholeness brings two people together, there is also a greater purpose involved. By greater purpose, I mean the positive contribution you can make to the world together that you couldn't make on your own. God wastes nothing in working out his master plan for humanity, not even relationships. The more whole we become, the brighter our light shines. When two whole lights come together, that brightness is multiplied and illuminates everyone around it.

Before meeting Sarah, I had a light and so did she. Today we still maintain our individual lights, but our union creates something even brighter. Our marriage is a demonstration of the power of love and purpose. It also represents to multitudes around the world the beauty and reality of God's restoration and brings hope and inspiration to them. It's important that you and your partner have at least a sense of what that greater purpose is. Talk about it intimately. Ask yourselves what each of you believes your purpose is and compare notes.

To come into a relationship as a whole light, you first need to be clear about your purpose as an individual. In fact, it is unwise to get married without knowing your purpose. Your purpose is what you have come to understand about God's direction for your life. You don't need to have every detail worked out, but you should have at least a hint about where you are headed before you commit yourself entirely to the life of another.

Your individual purpose must complement that of your beloved. Even if you have a lock on the other four must-have components of a relationship, if you can't achieve alignment on the greater purpose for your union, it likely means you aren't yet ready for marriage.

Everything in life has purpose, including and especially who you marry. Your purpose as an individual is a vital part of who you are and what you will become. It is unfair—to yourself and to your partner—to offer yourself in marriage when you haven't yet begun to discover yourself. Again, you don't have to have everything figured out; we will always be learning more about ourselves as we grow, and our purpose will evolve as we pursue it. Nevertheless, it is prudent to have at least a glimpse of where your ship is sailing before you decide to leave the dock with someone else.

The most rewarding and fulfilling relationships in life are those that involve two whole people. Contrary to what we learned in math, when it comes to relationships, two halves do not make a whole. Only whole individuals can create a whole marriage, and if the relationship is blessed by the God of wholeness, that's exactly what you can look forward to—and more.

CHAPTER 8

THOU SHALT KNOW THY PATTERNS

There is no way to escape the reality of patterns; it's how our world works. A pattern is any combination of qualities or factors that operate with consistency. If you look around right now, you will see things created by patterns. You may see a chair, a window, or even this book you're reading. When I look around, I see those things too, but when I look more deeply, I also see patterns. Functional chairs, windows, and books are all produced based on patterns that have proven effective. A similar dynamic applies to our internal patterns, which are simply our habits of thought and behavior. If we are serious about becoming whole, we must be aware of—and begin to see our life in terms of—patterns. The fruit of everything we create is the byproduct of patterns operating beneath the surface of our lives.

Because we are creatures of habit, we are predictable— often more than we realize. Corporations have figured this out and spend millions of dollars studying our patterns to determine our predictabilities. Numerous consulting firms have been started because technology makes it easier to recognize and identify what people do, when they do it, and why. The thought is that if they can discover our patterns, they can create the specific outcomes they desire, which typically include making a sale of some kind. If major corporations understand the significance of our patterns and spend so much money to identify them, surely we can prioritize knowing and regulating our patterns as we work toward the goal of becoming whole and attaining the lives we desire.

THE FRAMEWORK OF PATTERNS

Our patterns are composed of three things: our perceptions, our processing, and our reactions. These three dynamics operate in a cycle that produces the fruit, or outcome, of a pattern. Let's take a closer look at each one.

1. *Perceptions.* Our perceptions are what and how we see, and they are shaped by our experiences, our worldview, and our self-view. Our inner mirror plays a big part in our perceptions because it reflects our life back to us (more or less accurately, depending on how cracked it is). To illustrate, consider the experiences of two friends, Kayla and Chad, who walk into a crowded social gathering where they know no one. Kayla notices all the beautiful clothes people are wearing and

immediately feels intimidated. Chad notices the same beautiful clothes, but instead of being intimidated, he feels like these are people he'd like to meet and get to know better. It's the same situation for both Kayla and Chad, but their perceptions are very different.

2. *Processing.* Our processing is the inner mechanism that takes what we perceive and translates it into a storyline. The storyline communicates what the perception means to us or says about us. When Kayla processes her perceptions of the well-dressed people at the party, she develops a storyline that reinforces her perceptions: *Everyone here is better off than I am. I don't belong here, and I'm pretty sure they don't want me here either.* Chad's processing also leads to a storyline that reinforces his perceptions: *Everyone here looks so interesting! I can't wait to meet them and see what we have in common.*

3. *Reactions.* Our reactions are the actions we take in response to how we feel about what we perceive. Back at the party, Kayla's reaction to what she's perceived and processed is to declare that the party is boring, the people are stuck up, and she wants to go home. Chad, on the other hand, is just getting started. He's shaking hands, making friends, and can't figure out why Kayla is being such a wet blanket. This is a great party!

This is the framework of a pattern. As with Kayla and Chad, a pattern is always made up of how we perceive, process, and react. If you can understand and master this sequence of events and be intentional about doing the work necessary to ensure that your patterns are healthy, your life will thrive. And there is even more good news: you don't have to work on your patterns by yourself. The God of wholeness is on your side and will guide the way.

KNOWING YOURSELF

I marvel at how readily available information is today. What would have taken hours or even days of library research when I was a kid is now retrieved in a matter of seconds with a few keystrokes on a laptop or touches on a smartphone. We have access to information about everything you can imagine, from ancient history to astrophysics. We are perhaps the most knowledgeable generation of all time, except when it comes to the most important thing we could ever know—ourselves.

As much of a blessing as the information age has been, its downside is its power to distract us from truly knowing ourselves. We have become so reliant on the internet and social media that we hardly get to be "social" and acquainted with our own selves. We are well informed about the world around us but blinded to the happenings of the world within us.

The busyness of technology often robs us of the stillness needed to really know ourselves. Our focus shifts so fast—at the speed of a click—that our minds can hardly be still. Although we are feeling things all the time, if we never stop to be still, we can never identify and examine those feelings and what may be underneath. There is a whole world happening inside us that we don't see, which gives us no say in the outcomes that our inner world produces. Instead of making life happen, we allow life to happen to us through unseen patterns. We need to understand these patterns and master them.

TRUSTING THE PROCESS OF SELF-KNOWLEDGE

Whole people identify and manage their patterns by taking a regular inventory of their perceptions, processing, and reactions. This requires making a habit of solitude, stillness, self-examination, and soul-searching. The challenge is that too many of us don't know how to be alone and are afraid of what we may see if we spend any amount of time looking within. We've learned how to function in our dysfunction, and although we may not be operating at our full potential, at least we know that our present life is manageable. The thought of what we might find if we start dismantling the structure our life is standing on is frightening. We wonder, *Who might I become if I start digging around in the dark basement of my soul? What if I awaken a version of me I'm not equipped to deal with? Maybe things could be better by looking within, but what if it only makes my life worse? Maybe I should just take comfort in knowing that no one is perfect and just manage what's in front of me.* These are some of the all-too-common fears that keep us repeating the unhealthy patterns that limit our lives. But right on the other side of those fears is the life most of us only dream of having.

The starting point for spending time in quiet and self-reflection is the knowledge that you aren't really alone. As you look within, you do so in the loving presence of the God of wholeness, and there is no safer place you could be. When you are surrounded by pure love, you can look within yourself without fear or shame. Listen for the voice that says, "I've got you covered. I know you, and I'm with you. Trust me to walk you through this process. I'll take you step by step, and you will emerge victorious, new, and whole. I'm going to show you your life through my eyes so you can see who you are destined to be. When I look at you, I see much worth and great value. All you may see right now is impenetrable rock, but I see fine and rare gold. I just need you to be courageous and to trust me as we take this journey together."

The God of wholeness is invested in your becoming whole and has all of the resources in the universe and beyond at his disposal on your behalf. If you are willing to journey with him to discover your patterns, there is zero possibility of failure.

BECOMING TRACEABLE

Breaking unhealthy patterns is about awareness and change. If you are going to establish and maintain healthy patterns in your life, you must learn to become what I call traceable.

Being traceable means you have a system that allows you to trace, or track, the way you perceive, process, and react in any given situation. It is to be intentional about truly knowing yourself, including what you do and why you do it. Becoming traceable means you understand your predictabilities and, when necessary, take action to change them.

My process of making myself traceable is through always taking inventory of where I am and constantly asking myself a series of questions:

- "How are you? How do you feel, really?"
- "Are you confident, or are you feeling insecure?"
- "What thoughts are shaping your state of being?"
- "How long have you felt this way?"
- "You just reacted in an unusual way. What was that about, really?"

We often hear the phrase "keeping it real" in connection with how we relate to others, but we often fail to keep it real in how we relate to ourselves. The path to wholeness requires having a healthy relationship with yourself, a willingness to dig deep, and a commitment to constant self-reflection and self-examination.

I'd like to let you in on an unhealthy pattern I discovered in my own life, and what I did to turn my negative predictability into a positive one that enhanced my ability to maintain meaningful relationships with great people. But before I do, I want to give you a little bit of background.

I've always been a people person and relationships mean a lot to me, but I've also experienced considerable loss and unpredictability in my relational world; many people have come and gone in my life. First, there was the move from Northern California to Southern California when I was a boy. Then I switched schools several times as my neighborhood changed or my family's upward mobility allowed me to attend better schools. When I went to college, I left some relationships behind and established new ones. Then there was my eleven-year career in the corporate world, in which people and relationships were changing all the time. Perhaps the most dramatic change in my relationships happened when I left the business world to become a full-time minister. As beautiful as many of its expressions are, the Christian community does come with its occasional, shall I say, character. I'm sure I myself have been a character a time or two on my journey to wholeness! Let's just sum it all up by saying I had very few relationships that lasted beyond the time I spent in the neighborhood, the school environment, the workplace, or the church I was part of at the time.

My relationships with peers were also sometimes complicated by envious slights I often experienced. I had a unique aptitude for achievement and success, an outgoing personality, and—I humbly submit for your consideration—good looks. Beneath all these realities, I also had a difficult relationship with my father, one in which I experienced profound rejection. Given all this, you might be able to understand why relationships were a complex and often sensitive issue for me. So that's the background. Now let's get to the unhealthy pattern.

In my early thirties, I began to notice a pattern that involved my relationships with people I looked up to or admired in some way. Even though I had access to them, I was hesitant to reach out. When I did work up the nerve to contact someone, there would often be a delay in his or her response or no response at all. I would tell myself it wasn't a big deal and try to shake it off, but deep within, my attitude toward that person would change. I began to develop a negative perception and rejected that person as someone I wanted to be close to.

This pattern also played itself out on social media. I would follow people I looked up to, and if I didn't get a return follow in a reasonable amount of time, I would unfollow them. I did this for years, not recognizing that it was an unhealthy pattern that had nothing to do with the other person and everything to do with me. I'm going to tell you how I traced this pattern, but before I do, I want to look at the fruit, or outcome, of it.

There's a popular term in culture today—a hater. And that was the fruit of my unhealthy pattern: I was becoming a hater. A hater is someone who, well, hates. They don't like to see anyone but themselves succeed. They are fueled by pride, are extremely critical, and have only negative things to say about others. Some haters can be mean-spirited and cantankerous, and others just generally critical. But what I have learned after sipping my own cup of hatorade a time or two is that most haters are simply people who've been hurt, usually because of an unhealthy pattern that needs to be healed.

The unhealthy pattern in my life—rejecting people who didn't respond to me the way I hoped—had at times made me a hater, and I didn't like the feeling. It wasn't me at my best, and I knew it. Had this pattern persisted, it would have blocked blessings in my life and ruined relationships that were a part of my destiny. Developing the practice of tracing my patterns has become an irreplaceable discipline in my pursuit of wholeness, and the fruit has been tremendous. My relationships have become more authentic and rewarding as a result, and my more positive outlook has prospered all my endeavors in remarkable ways. I'm excited to see the same happen for you, so let's look deeper into mastering our patterns.

AUTOPSY THE FRUIT TO TRACE THE PATTERN

An unhealthy pattern always produces what I like to call dead fruit. Dead fruit is what is produced in a person's life as the result of an unhealthy pattern. The outcome is undesirable, unhealthy, and unbecoming. Dead fruit is always unpleasant, causes pain, and contaminates the soul. However, there is one redemptive benefit to dead fruit. If we are willing to take a closer look, it will reveal the source and cause of our unhealthy patterns. And by taking a closer look, I don't mean a quick glance. I mean a deep exploration intent on identifying the cause of death, which is precisely what an autopsy is.

This autopsy requires two parties: you, as the coroner,

and the God of wholeness, as the chief medical examiner who will assist you. If you are going to be healed from your unhealthy pattern, you must allow Wholeness to help you do this exploratory work. He has the expertise you'll need to solve the case.

For me, a big part of the unhealthy pattern that caused me to be a hater was pride. It was pride that led me to be critical of others I felt had rejected me, and it was self-protection motivated by pride that led me to bluff that I really didn't care about those people anyway. Pride is almost always a sign of unacknowledged or unprocessed hurt. When I recognized the pride, I knew I needed to ask more questions and dig deeper. "What feeling is my pride truly masking?" The answer came almost immediately: hurt.

The next question I needed to ask was, "Why do I feel hurt?" This was hard because pride was still trying to protect me by keeping me from actually admitting the hurt. But I also knew that pride couldn't help me at all in this process. If I wanted to identify the cause of death and trace my unhealthy pattern back to its source, I had to be vulnerable and honest. What hurt me was the rejection I felt when people I respected and admired failed to respond when I reached out. This admission alone was a big step for me. And I could do it only because I felt safe and secure in the loving presence of the God of wholeness. As hard as it is to do, a vulnerable admission is always a significant step. It is the sign that you are headed down the beautiful road to freedom, healing, and the release of a debilitating pattern.

Now that I had admitted that I felt rejection, I had to figure out where that perception came from. "Why do I feel rejected?" Before I continue tracing the pattern, it's important to acknowledge a valuable truth about rejection, which is this: there is a difference between someone rejecting you and your being a reject. You are never a reject. Never. In the eyes of God, you are only ever one thing, "the beloved." I like that term *beloved*. It not only describes who you and I are, but it also gives us permission to *be loved*. It's an invitation to accept the rich and unconditional love God has for us. So hear me on this: there is never a moment when you are anything but loved, accepted, rooted for, validated, and celebrated. It is possible that people may reject you from time to time, but always know that even when they do, *you* are never a reject. Your identity is and always will be the beloved. If someone rejects you, it simply means that they can't see you for who you are, usually because they don't yet know who they are. This truth about rejection is one I have been especially concerned to pass on to my fifteen-year-old son, Isaiah.

Isaiah is a budding actor, and before every audition I coach him by telling him something like this: "Now, Son, you know that you don't need anything from the people in that room that you don't already have. You are loved, accepted, provided for, protected, and destined for great things. You have all this before going into that room. You are there to give something, not to get. You are already full, so just go in there confident in these things and let your light shine. Everything else will take care of itself." After the audition, and regardless of how he feels about it, I stand up, give him a high-five, and tell him how proud I am of him. Then we head to the dessert venue of his choice to celebrate *him*, not the outcome of the audition. What I didn't realize when I first starting coaching my son this way was that I was modeling wholeness to him.

Okay, back to tracing my pattern. "Why do I feel rejected?" I realized that the rejection I felt was the narrative produced from my perceptions and my processing. Remember, the framework of a pattern involves a cycle of perceptions, processing, and reactions. When I didn't get the response I hoped for from the people I admired, I perceived rejection and therefore processed it into a narrative of rejection. My reaction was then to reject the people I perceived to have rejected me. Obviously, my reaction was problematic for a number of reasons, but let's take a closer look at my processing.

Anytime an individual failed to respond to my communication, my processor automatically assumed there could be only one explanation: willful disregard and rejection. The truth is that there could have been an unlimited number of other explanations, anything from technology glitches, hectic calendars, or personal priorities to the need for time to gather information to make a response more helpful—and the list could go on. The more I thought about it, the more likely it seemed that these people weren't rejecting me when they didn't respond. If that was the case, then why did my processor default to concluding rejection? Because my processing was connected to my perceptions.

As I mentioned in chapter 5, our perceptions determine

how we see life, ourselves, and others. My inner mirror had been cracked because of the sense of rejection I experienced in my relationship with my father, and then it was repeatedly cracked again over time when so many of my relationships were lost or fell apart. All these cracks distorted not only what I perceived in others but also how I processed my perceptions. It meant I could never look at potential relationships clearly. I always assumed my relationships would not work out because rejection and loss were inevitable. Because I felt rejectable, I could perceive others only as potential rejecters, so I automatically labeled them untrustworthy.

This negative outlook was the origin of my unhealthy pattern. After years of being robbed by it, I had finally traced and arrested the pattern by autopsying the dead fruit. Once I had uncovered the pattern's mechanics, there was only one thing left to do—change it.

BREAKING UNHEALTHY PATTERNS

Love, not condemnation or shame, is the source and the starting point for breaking unhealthy patterns. Knowing that I was the beloved enabled me to love myself, and it motivated me to know myself more intimately. I was determined to figure out how I was operating in self-defeating ways, so I could make the changes that would enable me to live my one and only life to the fullest. I was fully committed to my wholeness.

By tracing my unhealthy pattern to its source, I was able

to put together a strategy to overcome it. It was a strategy that began with the discipline of listening to my heart. This meant routinely setting aside time to be still so I could be in touch with what I was feeling. In times past, I allowed the busyness of life to drown out my feelings. Now I had decided that this way of living was no longer tolerable.

When I attended to my heart and listened to what it had to say, I started receiving honest feedback. When my heart felt sick, I invited Wholeness in to heal it. When my heart noticed the hater within arising, I went on a diligent search for the faulty processing that was creating that reaction. And the more I listened to my heart, the stronger this new pattern became. Instead of requiring a lot of effort, tracing my unhealthy patterns back to their source simply became a routine part of my operating system. Once I could identify the negative perceptions and processing, all I had to do was renounce that narrative and replace it with the highest thought about anyone I perceived had wronged me.

Perhaps the most important thing I needed to regularly work on to strengthen this new and healthy pattern was my perceptions. Especially in the beginning, I needed to pay close attention to ensure that I was viewing myself from the perspective of wholeness, not brokenness. I knew that my sense of personal identity would always be the starting point for my patterns. If my self-perception was healthy, I was much more likely to enjoy healthy patterns and the rewards that follow. If my self-perception was unhealthy, unhealthy patterns would continue to form and need to be addressed.

Recognizing that I couldn't always trust my perceptions, I decided to let Wholeness coach me on how to see myself, how to see others, and what to expect out of this life. Wholeness's commentary on all these things was always positive and true. Wholeness affirmed my value by calling me royalty. Wholeness taught me that others are royalty too but often don't know it. Wholeness instructed me to believe the best in others, and if I did, he would often bring out the best in them. When people disappointed me, Wholeness told me to forgive them quickly—multiple times if necessary—and not to believe the lie that they would never change. Wholeness made plain to me that this didn't mean I should forego wisdom and caution; it only meant that I should keep an open mind about them, because with Wholeness anything is possible. Wholeness also taught me that the healthiest way to perceive life is to expect good out of it. That didn't mean there wouldn't be tests and trials in life, because these are guaranteed. It just meant that I could be optimistic, joyful, and courageous in spite of them, because Wholeness had already gone ahead of me, overcoming every obstacle I would face.

As long as I allowed Wholeness to keep my perceptions healthy, my processing improved, and I began to notice healthier reactions and better results in my relationships. It was truly life changing! I had learned a new pattern, and this time the fruit was sweet. My old patterns didn't change overnight—I had to work at it—but they did change. And the same is possible for you. You'll have to work the new pattern until it replaces the old, and even when the new pattern becomes more established, you still can't let down your guard. We call them patterns for a reason: they like to keep coming back! Tracing patterns is a lifelong process, but it produces lifelong rewards.

ON THE OTHER SIDE OF WHY

In our efforts to practice self-awareness and reveal unhealthy patterns, perhaps the most powerful question we can ask is, "Why?" This question shines light on all the things we just do without thinking. Asking myself why I felt hurt when I didn't hear back from people is what led to a significant breakthrough. Asking why again helped me continue tracing my pattern back to its source. Asking why enabled me to see my underlying motivation. What really mattered wasn't so much what I was doing (my reactions) but why I was doing it (my perceptions and processing). Knowing my patterns meant asking the question why about everything I did, to discover the truth about why I did it. Inevitably, my motivation revealed the source of the problem.

One year for my birthday, I bought myself an expensive watch. Without question, the watch was beautiful, stylish, and trendy, but over time I realized the watch had come to represent more than a fashion statement. When I'm at home on my days off, my standard uniform is sweats, a T-shirt, and tennis shoes. I started to notice that when I left the house to run a simple errand or two, I always put on my expensive watch. So there I would be, in the grocery store or at the dry cleaners, wearing my casual clothes and my expensive watch. I did it for years but never asked myself why. One day, after feeling something about wearing it, I was brave enough to ask myself, "Why do I feel the need to wear my fancy watch whenever I am dressed down?" My honest answer: "Because I don't want to be perceived as poor or less than people I may encounter." Now, at first glance, this reason might seem a little self-conscious but maybe not so bad. It's just a young man taking pride in himself and showing off his hard work, right? Not quite. Getting to the truth meant digging deeper.

To find the unhealthy pattern, I had to ask another why: "Why is it important to me not to be perceived as inferior to someone I may run into?" It was my response to this question that helped me identify that there was a problem with my perception of self, my processing about how others perceived me, and my pride-based reaction, which was crying out, "Look at me—I'm equal to you!" The fruit was a false sense of self-worth and value, one based not on my identity as the beloved but on a material item.

By asking two whys, I had uncovered a doozy. It was an unhealthy pattern that nurtured my insecurities. By attaching my self-worth to a watch that I thought would earn me affirmation and acceptance, I was putting myself in bondage. As long as this unhealthy pattern went undetected, I would be a slave to it, constantly trying and failing to use material things to fill a void only Wholeness could fill. Needless to say, as soon as I recognized what was happening, I stopped wearing the watch when I left the house in my sweats. But more important, I surrendered my perceptions and processing to Wholeness so my life could be healed and changed. That's when I discovered how liberating it was to walk around without feeling like I needed to prove anything to anyone. It was freedom! Then I began to wonder how much money that pattern had cost me over the years. I quickly moved on from that line of thinking, because it almost made me nauseous. Best to leave the past in the past and just be grateful that I'm better now.

What about you? Where do you need to ask, "Why?" What patterns in your life are aiding and abetting your brokenness and keeping you from the freedom of wholeness? Are you willing to take the time to be still enough to feel your feelings, to listen to your heart? If you quiet yourself, look and listen, you will discover the clues that will help you trace your patterns to their source. You have an inner mechanism that determines the fruit of your life—your perceptions, your processing, and your reactions. To become whole, you have to know yourself intimately and always be willing to question your actions. As you develop new ways of perceiving, processing, and reacting, you'll experience major shifts in your life. And when that happens, the things you once thought were impossible might well become possible after all. Take Wholeness by the hand and run forward. You are becoming unstoppable.

PART 3

THE JOURNEY CONTINUES

CHAPTER 9

STEP BY STEP

It's important to remember that the pursuit of wholeness is a journey—a long one. In fact, it lasts a lifetime. There will be times when you experience such significant breakthroughs that you might think, *It can't get any better than this. I've arrived!* But the truth is, for every mountaintop you reach, there is a new mountain yet to climb—a mountain that is taller, steeper, and more difficult to navigate. But don't worry. Everything you learned on the last mountain prepares you to conquer the next one.

I share this truth about the long-haul nature of becoming whole not to discourage you but to inform you, so you aren't surprised when becoming whole takes longer than you think it should. If we could, all of us would probably choose to be the best version of ourselves overnight. But that's not how the process of growth and healing works. It takes time to work through brokenness that runs deep and then gets deeper as life goes on. There is no instant fix for that.

The process of becoming whole also requires all of our life experiences, the good and the bad. All of it is raw material for creating something beautiful out of our brokenness. Earlier in the book, I likened the process of becoming whole to that of a master potter shaping a prized creation. When a potter spins his wheel, he is creating the movement that enables him to alter, define, and refine the shape of the vessel he is creating. We too require a fair amount of movement as Wholeness molds us into shape. Life brings a myriad of experiences, some pleasant and others painful. Wholeness uses both—in fact needs both—to create a masterpiece of us.

THE THREE DYNAMICS OF BECOMING WHOLE

The overarching process of becoming whole can be broken down into three primary dynamics: being altered, being defined, and being refined. Each happens on the potter's wheel during the turns of life. Let's look at them one by one.

Altered

The moment the potter touches the clay, he begins working it with his hands to make it pliable. Without pliability, the clay will never become what the potter envisions. The same is true for you and me as we pursue wholeness. This process of change is never easy. In fact, we might wish for an entirely different kind of process, like a digital one. Wouldn't it be cool if we could just download wholeness? You could click a button and be instantly upgraded to the new version of yourself—YOU 2.0. As nice as that would be, I'm pretty sure it's never going to happen. There are no shortcuts to wholeness, and the slow and steady process of change is a fundamental requirement for getting there.

Most of us want to see changes in our lives but are uncomfortable with actually changing. We don't like the discomfort of feeling undone, exposed, or uncertain, so our first response to being altered is often to resist it. But what's required at this point is just the opposite. Instead of resisting the alteration process, we need to submit to it.

Just imagine. You're sitting there on the shelf with all the other clay, when the potter suddenly selects you and places you on the wheel. You've admired the finished works the potter created, but you've never seen the process that transformed those objects from lumps of clay into masterpieces. You feel a little nervous, but you also feel excited about what you might become. Until the spinning begins.

Not only is the world now spinning beyond recognition, but the potter is digging his fingers into you, pushing and pulling you this way and that. Everything about you that once felt firm and secure is being undone in unfamiliar and uncomfortable ways. Despite what you've seen of the potter's work, you begin to suspect that far from being transformed into a masterpiece, you are being deformed into something unrecognizable. It occurs to you that you would probably be much better off just sitting on the shelf with all the other lumps of clay than going through these uncomfortable alterations. But then you notice something. You're getting softer, and the pushing and pulling no longer feels so uncomfortable.

You begin to relax a little, trusting that maybe the potter knows what he's doing after all.

Oh, to be like clay! In the potter's hands, we are destined to become a masterpiece. But we have to be determined to stay there. Why? Because unlike clay, when the altering process gets difficult, we can jump off the potter's wheel and go back to the shelf. The altering process is a tough part of the journey to wholeness, but it's essential. This is where we become pliable and soft, ready for shaping into something new. If you choose to lean into this process rather than resist it—if you let Wholeness do the work that only a master potter can do—I can promise you that your new form will soon begin to take shape.

Defined

I'll be honest: what I love most about the altering phase is when it ends, when the pushing and pulling finally stops and it's time to move on to being defined. The definition phase is when we begin to take on our new shape.

The process of being made pliable and soft wasn't easy, but now you begin to feel yourself becoming something new. Your new form feels lighter, more beautiful. Instead of feeling deformed, you actually feel more like who you really are and wonder how you ever could have settled for being a lump of clay. In fact, you're now so excited about what you are becoming that you are even more responsive to the potter's hands. What once felt like change gone wrong now feels like the best thing that ever happened to you.

Just as a potter envisions what the clay on his wheel has the potential to become, Wholeness knows the beautiful shape you will take when you are healed and whole. At this point in the process, the rotations on the potter's wheel take you through the following cycle:

1. *Identifying* is recognizing the self-defeating patterns that keep you from progressing in life.
2. *Confronting* is facing the unhealthy patterns you've identified. You decide that these patterns cannot and will not continue, because you will no longer partner with anything that keeps you from moving forward and becoming whole.
3. *Extracting* is unearthing the self-defeating patterns, pulling them out by the roots so they can no longer grow in your life.
4. *Planting* introduces new and healthy patterns where the old ones were extracted. It is never wise to leave open spaces where dysfunctional weeds once grew. Doing so runs the risk of more-aggressive weeds returning, causing even more problems than the first ones.
5. *Healing* takes place after the new patterns are planted and established, and leads to a new level of wholeness.

At the end of this process, you are no longer the person you once were. A real change has happened, and you know it. Things that used to trip you up no longer do. You've moved past the altering phase and have been defined on the potter's wheel. You went from stiff and formless to soft and pliable, from soft and pliable to a whole new shape. And the good news is, it gets even better from here.

Refined

Being altered makes you pliable, being defined gives you shape, and being refined makes you a masterpiece. The master potter always begins with a beautiful vision in mind and will not stop refining his creation until every detail of his vision is achieved. In the same way, Wholeness is not finished with us just because we experience a wonderful breakthrough or two. Wholeness is far from finished with us.

I had the privilege of counseling a young businessman who was having some challenges in his marriage. By and large, he was a phenomenal husband, a great leader, and had been healed from tremendous brokenness in his life. The problem was that he and his wife couldn't find common ground in their sex life. He wanted to be intimate with her all the time—literally. If they were home together in bed, regardless of their energy level or interest, he couldn't go to sleep without having sex and would urge his wife to accommodate him. Although she wanted to be responsive, there were times when she just could not bear his untimely advances. This created a tension in their marriage they couldn't seem to get past, until he reached out to me for help.

In our initial conversation, he described how he was raised in a single-parent family with a mom who didn't show affection very well. His mother worked long hours to make ends meet, and there were many times as a young boy when he was left at home alone. Without a father in the house, his mother became his hero. The only problem was that his hero didn't express love in a way that he could recognize or receive. As he grew older, he became promiscuous and ultimately fell into a lifestyle of sexual addiction. Fortunately, he eventually experienced healing and then settled down and got married. He loved his wife, and it really bothered him that they couldn't get on the same page regarding sex.

After listening to his history and asking him questions about what sex meant to him, I was pretty sure I had figured out the root of his problem. His desire for sex wasn't about lust; it was about connection. His mother's absence and lack of affection created brokenness in his life at an early age. His promiscuity was an attempt to experience the love and affection he had longed for. Although he had been healed of his addiction on one level and no longer lived a promiscuous lifestyle, he still needed to be made whole on the next level and in a deeper way. He needed to be refined.

The issue that was frustrating his marriage had little to do with his marriage. It was an unresolved internal issue that his marriage unearthed. Once we traced the problem back to the root, extracted it, and planted in its place a new truth about his mother's love, he was able to experience a deeper level of healing. When he emerged from this refining cycle, he was a new man all over again and could experience life and marriage in a healthier, more rewarding way.

No matter how far we travel up the mountain of our potential, we must never deceive ourselves into thinking there's nothing left to overcome. It's something like cleaning up an area where a glass has fallen and shattered—which, by the way, is one of my least favorite chores. No matter how carefully I sweep and scan the floor for broken pieces, it seems like I always miss at least one. Just when I think I'm finished, I catch a glimpse of another small piece of glass that somehow managed to travel all the way to the other side of the room. If I weren't committed to looking everywhere and getting every last shard, I or someone I love could get hurt. That's the attitude we must have when pursuing wholeness.

A BEAUTIFUL MESS

As challenging as it is to stay on the potter's wheel, you must remain committed. This is critical to reaching your full potential. Believe me, I know all too well the work it takes to remain in progress. I've had many experiences in this area! Allow me to bring you into one that challenged me to the core. My path to wholeness in this instance wasn't pretty, but the healing that emerged when it was all said and done was undeniably worth it.

One day, after attending a rigorous kickboxing fitness class, I experienced intense pain in my right shoulder. It wasn't the first time my shoulder had given me trouble, but this time the pain was much worse. Most of the time when I had shoulder pain during a workout, I didn't think it was any-thing serious. Once I took a break and rested, I could return to working out another day. In fact, that's how things had been for at least two decades. I simply accepted this condition as normal and went on with my life. But this particular day, I couldn't just move on. Even after I stopped working out, the pain continued and even worsened.

After talking the situation over with my wife, I made an appointment with my doctor the same day, and he sent me directly to the hospital for X-rays. After the first X-ray had been taken, the technician asked if I had ever had surgery on my shoulder. What the technician clearly saw on the X-ray was something I had blocked from my memory—shrapnel across my right shoulder blade.

When I was sixteen and living in inner-city Los Angeles, I was the victim of a drive-by shooting. While I was driving home from a fast-food restaurant, a vehicle pulled up alongside mine, a brief exchange ensued, and within a matter of seconds I had been shot. The bullet entered near my right shoulder blade, bounced off, and then traveled up until it lodged in my throat. By God's grace, I survived the physical injury, but in the years that followed, I somehow blocked out the memory of it.

My response to the technician's question was quick and defensive: "Oh yeah, I got shot there when I was sixteen years old."

Immediately, I felt an old familiar feeling. It was the same feeling I'd had when I was trying to pretend I wasn't hurt when my father canceled the fishing trip I had planned. *Uh-oh,*

I thought. *There is something broken beneath the surface.* Then I felt anxious.

My entire disposition changed when my previous injury was discovered. I felt ashamed and extremely self-conscious about being shot. What would these medical professionals think of me? What type of person gets shot? Maybe they would think I was some sort of drug dealer or thug. As a black male, I knew I could easily be stereotyped. I remember reaching into my treasure chest of words and trying hard to impress the doctors with my extensive vocabulary and intelligence. Yet, even in the midst of it all, I knew there was brokenness within that I needed to address—and soon.

This was a brokenness I never knew existed, and I wasn't ready to face it. I was afraid of what I might discover if I took a closer look. Things were going very well in my life. I was close to closing a partnership deal with a major television network. I was being invited to speak all around the country. My family and I had just moved into our beautiful new home, and our church and businesses were all beginning to thrive. I didn't want to jeopardize any of that by having a personal crisis. But I knew I had to make a choice: address the brokenness or stuff it back down and try to keep moving forward with my life. It definitely would have been easier to just get lost in all the outer success, but in my heart I knew better. If I chose not to address what was going on inside me, my *life* might continue to prosper, but Touré would not. To be whole, I had to go through the messy yet beautiful process of confronting my brokenness.

As I began to process the experience of being shot, I realized I had blocked the memory not so much because of the physical trauma but because of how devaluing the incident was. There was a cold and lifeless look in the eyes of the men who shot me. My life meant nothing at all to them. I wasn't even worthy of their anger. In fact, I believe it would have been less traumatic to me if they had been angry. But their cold, emotionless silence conveyed that my life wasn't worth even the energy of anger. Greater than the pain of the bullet that entered my body that night was the pain of the one that entered my soul. Getting shot that way was the most devaluing thing that had ever happened to me.

After working through the shooting step by step and thought by thought, I realized how failing to process the experience in the light of truth caused it to be ill-processed. I blocked the memory because I had processed the experience into a false narrative that said getting shot was shameful and devaluing. But the truth was that getting shot was nothing to be ashamed of. And it certainly had nothing to do with my value or worth. If anything, the incident was more of a statement about how the perpetrators perceived their own value and worth. Through their violence, they projected onto me the shame they felt and the lack of worth they placed on their own lives. The incident was never about my value; it was always about theirs.

As Wholeness was leading me to these truths, I began to identify with people who had experienced other kinds of trauma, particularly sexual trauma. Many survivors feel shame about being abused and even blame themselves for what happened to them. But being a victim never makes us responsible for our trauma. We didn't do anything wrong. We don't need to be ashamed, and what happened can't ever take away our value. We are never made damaged goods because of what we endure in life. Even if we experience damaging things, when we allow Wholeness to rewrite the false narratives we've told ourselves, the most damaging experiences can be healed and redeemed for our good.

Becoming whole is a long journey, one that continues for a lifetime. There is always a new mountain to climb. As we ascend from one mountaintop to the next, we will discover new layers of brokenness we have to examine and work through. As it was with me when my shoulder injury was discovered, there will also be a temptation to shrink back when pain rears its ugly head. But shrinking back doesn't make the brokenness go away. It just postpones the battle for another day, allowing our brokenness to gain momentum.

To become whole and to maximize your potential, you must embrace the messy but beautiful process of change. If you do the work, each time a stronger and healthier version of you will emerge. Always stay pliable and soft. Trust the process and allow yourself to be shaped into a masterpiece. Wholeness is still at work, and the best and most beautiful you is yet to come.

CHAPTER 10

GHOSTS OF THE PAST

You may not yet be able to fully grasp it, but you have an unrivalled ally in Wholeness. Wholeness doesn't start you on the journey only to abandon you when things get ugly. Wholeness came into your life because of the ugly and won't quit working in your life until everything in it is made beautiful. This doesn't mean things will always happen easily. In fact, many times you will have to fight for your own wholeness. However, you can take courage in knowing that Wholeness has prequalified you to conquer every obstacle you face on your journey. The very presence of an obstacle is proof you can defeat it.

Perhaps the most challenging obstacle we all face on the journey to wholeness is this beast called the past. While the voice of Wholeness invites you forward into a better and healthier future, the voice of your past beckons you backward into memories that only haunt you. Just to clarify, I do believe there are healthy ways to learn from the past, such as gleaning wisdom by reflecting on mistakes to avoid repeating them. This is a profitable use of the past because it adds value to your present and future. However, there is also an unhealthy engagement with the past that can derail your present and your future. Sooner or later, the ghosts of your past sneak up on you and try to drag you backward.

Ghosts of the past might come in a variety of forms. Sometimes you'll experience them as a yearning for the comfort or perceived safety of life as it used to be, even though life as it used to be was not healthy or whole. Other times you'll feel weighted down by painful regrets, or deep grief over the loss of relationships. You may also wonder if that something you overcame in the past is suddenly going to reemerge and threaten your present or sabotage your future. To stay on your path to wholeness, you need to be prepared for these sometimes-vicious attacks by the ghosts of the past.

GHOST 1: YEARNING FOR YESTERDAY

I'm thoroughly convinced that one of the most pointless uses of energy is yearning for a time that doesn't exist anymore. I don't want to appear insensitive here, especially when it comes to memories of special moments we have all experienced in life. Those are priceless treasures we can and should hold near and dear in our hearts. What I am speaking to is more of an obsessive nostalgia that causes you to yearn for a time in your life that no longer exists. When this happens, it's a sign that the ghosts of the past are at your door, and you need to send them packing. In order to experience the power of the present moment, you have to be fully present in that moment. And if your power and energy is spent longing for the past, you forfeit the power to create a future that's even better.

There is a reason why your past doesn't outlive you. It's because your past isn't equipped to handle who you are becoming. You're here today because you were made for the now. There is something about you that now needs, and there is something about now that you need. To yearn for the past is like walking through life backward, only ever looking at where you've been. If you would just turn around, you would see even greater things on the horizon.

In my own life, I discovered an interesting pattern connected to my yearning for the past. I longed for yesterday only when I felt discouraged, anxious, or uncertain about the present. When I felt confident and certain of my purpose, the past held no attraction for me. That's when I realized that my longing for the past was really about fear. This epiphany helped me to realize that my feelings of nostalgia were an illusion, an attempt to escape whatever unpleasant emotions I was feeling in the present. Longing for the past was a sign that I needed to pause and remind myself that everything I truly wanted was in the present and the future. I reminded myself of all the progress I'd made, all the obstacles I'd already overcome, and the numerous confirmations that the God of wholeness was with me and was still guiding me up the mountain.

Even if you could go back to yesterday, you wouldn't fit there anymore. The past worked for you only because of who you were then. You're not the same person anymore, though nostalgia may try to convince you otherwise. Have you ever gone back to visit a place where you once lived or a school you once attended? You were all excited to go back, but when you got there, the place seemed so much different than you remembered. In your fond memories, it was bigger, happier, or more beautiful. But now that you're back, it feels smaller and unfamiliar. Although you have happy memories, you can't envision the present version of you ever fitting in there again. I've had many experiences like that.

The life of progress we all are called to live guarantees we will forever be outgrowing our past. It's okay to look back and smile from time to time, but the greatest joys aren't in our rearview; they are on the horizon, yet to be reached.

GHOST 2: REGRET

There probably isn't a person alive today who doesn't have at least one thing in their past they wish they could change. This is a common human experience, and if it hasn't happened to you yet, just keep living and you'll see what I mean. No one is perfect, which means we are guaranteed to make mistakes in life. Some of those errors are of minimal consequence, and some of greater consequence. The feelings of wishing we had done things differently are normal, but when those feelings lead to shame—because we can't separate what we did from who we are—we cross over into an unhealthy and self-defeating mindset called regret.

There are many things about regret that make it unhealthy and disruptive to our journey to wholeness. To begin with, regret is the lack of self-forgiveness in its purest form. When you have regret, there is a part of you that not only hates what you did but hates yourself for doing it. It imputes on you a life sentence without the possibility for parole. You never get out of failure jail because you deem yourself worthy of lifelong punishment. There is no life in regret, and nothing positive can come out of it. In fact, in my experience of counseling people through toxic regret, the only thing that comes out of a preoccupation with mistakes and failure are more mistakes and failure. And when people can't or won't see past what they've done, how can they ever truly expect to do something different?

Regret is like a cancer that eats people alive. To regret is to constantly grieve something we cannot change. Many times, the damage of regret is greater than the damage from the situation causing the regret. This is in no way to justify a wrongdoing. Wrong is wrong, and there is no way around it. Regret is a problem, but remorse is productive—and there is a clear difference between the two. To experience remorse is to grieve the wrong we have done, acknowledge that wrong, and then make a decision to change. Remorse says, "I was wrong, but I learned my lesson, and I will redeem my mistake by making better choices in the future." With remorse, our mistakes are a catalyst for change that helps us move forward. With regret, our mistakes are a ball and chain that keeps us anchored to the past.

Regret charges the present you with what a past version of

you did. Think about it. You aren't the same person now that you were when you made that unfortunate choice. If you were the same person, you wouldn't wish you could undo what you did. The grief you feel about it now proves that it was a past version of you who did it. When you condemn yourself, you're essentially charging an innocent person with the crimes of a person who no longer exists. You've grown and changed, and it isn't fair to the person you have become to remain in chains for the sins of your past self. That's the beauty of wholeness: it truly makes all things new.

This process gets complicated when there are people on the other end of your mistake, especially when it involves those who haven't come to the place of forgiveness. Forgiveness is one of the hardest things we can choose to do in life and, sadly, there are some who would rather die holding on to offenses they suffered than forgive them. It is possible that people affected by your mistake won't recognize or respect the reality of your transformation. Whenever possible, you should seek to win the forgiveness of those you've offended or wronged, but your freedom and self-forgiveness should never depend on whether someone else can forgive you. Do all you can to make peace, but never allow someone else's prison to become your own.

Say Goodbye to Regret

You've probably ascertained by now that I'm not a big fan of regret. You're right, and I'm not a fan for good reason. I had my own bout with regret and spent years tormented by it. All of my should haves, would haves, and could haves kept me from seeing what I did have. Regret disoriented me, keeping me from seeing the glorious life that was happening right in front of me. Once I realized how much my regret was costing—and calculated it against the value it was adding—I was astonished by the deficit. Doing business with regret was a bad deal, so I canceled the contract.

As soon as I released myself from the clutches of regret, my life began to change. The first thing I noticed was a dramatic shift in my confidence. I began to live more boldly and had a fresh wave of optimism about my future. I stopped playing life safe, made choices that took me out of my comfort zone, and started dreaming of greatness again. I learned that while I was preoccupied with condemning myself and mourning things I thought I'd lost, Wholeness had been working hard to restore those things, and most times even better things. These blessings had been available to me the entire time; I just had to get regret out of the way to experience them.

Through my own journey to the other side of regret, I discovered a five-step process that I believe will empower you to say goodbye to your own regrets once and for all. If you are willing to work this process, a tremendous weight will be removed from your life, leaving you better positioned for a promising and healthy future.

1. *Understand what regret is and the harm it causes.*
Make a clear distinction between remorse and regret: remorse enables you to move forward, but regret

chains you to the past. Don't indulge thoughts of regret and self-condemnation. Instead remind yourself that you are not defined by your past, and forgive yourself. You are not what you did.

2. *Take an inventory of what regret has cost you.* Get out a pen and a pad of paper. At the top of the page, write, "What Regret Has Cost Me." Then make a list. What did you miss out on in the present because regret kept you focused on the past? For starters, consider how regret may have siphoned off your creativity, your peace of mind, your optimism, and your ability to see the blessings right in front of you. Remember, regret adds no value to your life, so it's a terrible waste of energy and time.

3. *Choose to love and forgive yourself.* You *can* make the choice to love and forgive yourself. Pursuing wholeness means moving forward, and you can't do that if you are determined to punish yourself for the past. Remember, Wholeness wants to restore you, having already factored in the mistakes you have made along the way. If Wholeness loves you, accepts you, and believes the best for you, it's time for you to do the same.

4. *Create a do-over whenever possible.* There are times when you may be able to remedy the consequences of your mistake. Exhaust every option to do so, but only after releasing yourself from regret. If it involves making amends, be humble, gracious, and sincere,

but don't allow your peace, self-love, or sense of worthiness to be dependent on another's response. If you made a poor decision, make a new decision that sets you back on the right course. If your mistake was one of omission—failing to do something you wish you had done—what's keeping you from doing it now? Releasing yourself from regret doesn't mean you shouldn't try to fix what was broken. There are few things in life more beautiful than redemption, reconciliation, and restoration.

5. *Move on.* Separate who you are from what you did. It's time to turn your back on it. You don't live there anymore. So when you find yourself pulling into the driveway of regret, remember: it's not your home now. Regret was the land of bondage. Wholeness, the land of promise, is your new home.

GHOST 3: PEOPLE OF THE PAST

Sometimes the ghost of the past that haunts you is a lost relationship, with a person or a community. For one reason or another, the people you once assumed would be in your life forever are gone. You might miss them or feel troubled that things ended the way they did. This is a perplexing reality for anyone who sets out on a journey to wholeness. Not everyone you start with will be with you when you finish.

On my own journey, I began to notice that every season

of progress in my life seemed to include a relational casualty. The higher I climbed up the mountain, the fewer relationships I was able to retain. However, the quality of the relationships I did retain increased, and I eventually came to understand why.

For the most part, relationships are a reflection of where and who you are at a given time. The more whole you become, the more likely it is that your relationships will reflect that transformation. We attract what we are, so when we change, so do our relationships. This doesn't mean that when you grow, you automatically have to say goodbye to your friends. However, it does mean that in order to survive, any relationship you have will need to be able to grow with you. Every relationship that cannot evolve will soon dissolve. Wholeness qualifies what every relationship is at its core.

Perhaps you've heard the expression that relationships are for a reason, for a season, or for a lifetime. We may wish that all our relationships could achieve lifetime status, but that's not usually the case. Endings are just as necessary as beginnings. In fact, you can't have a new beginning without an ending. This is a truth you must embrace, and failing to do so will leave you longing for something that your destiny needed to let go of.

We never want to find ourselves reaching back into the past to water things that can no longer grow in our lives. That's what we do when we become obsessed with lost relationships. Instead water the new relationships Wholeness has placed in your life. Learn to celebrate them and enjoy the beauty they produce.

GHOST 4: THE BOOGEYMAN WHO NEVER COMES

This final ghost of the past is more fear than reality. It's the fear that the brokenness you've been freed from is going to reach into your future one day and cause trouble. That's why I call it the boogeyman who never comes. It's the threat of what might happen that leaves you afraid of *what if* and prevents you from enjoying the blessings of *what is*. You become so preoccupied with wondering whether you are going to make it that you fail to consider that you *are* making it.

If you're on the journey to wholeness, it's time to let go of the fear of the boogeyman who never comes. If the God of wholeness has brought you this far, don't you think he can bring you all the way to the finish line? And why would you want to spend your limited time and energy fearing some sort of retaliation from your past, when you could be diligently working toward your future? Don't sabotage your destiny because of a boogeyman that exists only in your mind.

Ghosts of the past are just that—ghosts. They're dead. The only power dead things have is the power you give them. So don't empower them. Don't let them steal your energy, your creativity, your optimism, or the current blessings in your life. It's time to say goodbye to the ghosts and hello to your future. When your past is your master, your future is in chains. But when Wholeness is your master, your future is limitless.

CHAPTER 11

THE THEOLOGY OF WHOLENESS

My introduction to everything I've learned about the God of wholeness happened in church. I was nine years old when my mother first took me there, primarily to expose me to faith, spirituality, and the tenets of good character. She was raising me by herself in a neighborhood where drugs, gangs, and all sorts of crime were just blocks away. Up against odds like those, she thought it best to get me involved with church, and she was right. I felt something powerful there. It was something bigger than me, and I knew it. I didn't understand everything I was experiencing, but I knew it was divine and that I needed it in my life, forever.

The people I went to church with never used the word wholeness or talked much about being whole except when they talked about people in the Bible who were healed from sickness. They talked about God, the creator of the heavens and the earth. They talked about Jesus, the Son of God, who came into this world to end the power of sin. And they talked about the Holy Spirit, whose purpose was to comfort us, lead us, and empower us to change. Not fully understanding all that I was being taught, I embraced what I could comprehend and began my spiritual journey. It wasn't until years later that I gained a deeper understanding of the connection between the God of wholeness and the faith I had embraced in church as a child.

When I was in my late twenties, I felt divinely urged to delve deeper into the faith of my childhood. I realized that God wanted more for me than simply being a "Christian." He wanted me to be whole—just like him—in every way. This was a significant awakening for me that not only changed the trajectory of my life but deepened both my relationship with God and my understanding of what God desires for us all. I learned that what God wants for us can be summed up in one word—wholeness.

Although I don't remember ever hearing the word wholeness in the church I grew up in, I do remember hearing another word quite often—holiness. I never put the two terms together, because the way holiness was used suggested being pious, not being whole and complete. The word holiness was used to relate to our actions. I learned that living a life of holiness meant refraining from any act or behavior considered unholy or unrighteous. This limited perspective on the concept of holiness overlooks a powerful reality about wholeness. To expect pious behavior externally from a person who isn't becoming whole internally is like expecting the cart to show up before the horse. It won't happen. God's process of making us whole is his guarantee that whole or holy actions will follow.

Right *doing* was never more important to God than right *being*. That's because God's plan for us is change. If an individual does what he or she feels are right things but never becomes God's idea of a right person, God's goal is not reached. God wants to see a version of us that reflects his own likeness, and as he guides us to that identity, holy actions naturally follow. I'll explain this process in more detail later, but for now we need to take a closer look at the identity of the God of wholeness.

THE GOD OF WHOLENESS

Wholeness has three unique expressions that work in sync to ensure that we become everything we are destined to be. Here is where I discovered that what I learned in church was much deeper and more profound than I had realized. In this section I want to bring you intimately into my spiritual journey and how I came to understand and define the path to wholeness. It may not be your path or belief system at the moment, and perhaps you'll never see it exactly the way I do. At the end of the day, we all have to work out our faith, and it requires a personal encounter with God. Nevertheless, I would be disingenuous if I didn't reveal to you the underpinnings of all of the truths and principles about wholeness—and Wholeness—that you have been reading in this book. Here's my story:

God the Everlasting Father

In church, I learned about God the Father, who created the world and everything in it. The most distinct attribute that this almighty God embodies is holiness. There are accounts in the Bible of angelic beings assembled around God's throne whose sole purpose is to proclaim, "Holy, Holy, Holy!" This is both praise for and the proclamation of God's identity. God is holy, which means that God is whole in every way. There is no brokenness in God, nor will there ever be. God is complete, lacks nothing, and is entirely self-sufficient. God is the embodiment of wholeness. There is nothing God wants more than to see wholeness realized in all of creation, including his beloved children. Furthermore, God not only desires our wholeness but provided a way for us to experience it through Jesus.

Jesus the Sacrificial Son

Jesus, the Son of God the Father, came into the world to be broken so that humanity could be healed. Growing up, I never doubted this was true, but it wasn't until much later that I understood the power of his substitution. I understood his dying on the cross for my brokenness, but I didn't realize that he had actually become my brokenness. By becoming brokenness itself, he had put brokenness to death so that through him, I could become whole like God. Jesus' resurrection was a powerful declaration of victory over humanity's brokenness, since he had conquered everything that once had the power to keep us broken.

Because Jesus had overcome every obstacle to wholeness, through him I had a clear path not only to heaven but to becoming whole.

The Holy Spirit

Learning about the Holy Spirit was a little more complicated for me than learning about God and Jesus. In the church tradition I grew up in, during the worship service people would "experience the Holy Spirit" in ways that sometimes confused me. In response to the message or one of the songs, they might begin to jump, call out in a loud voice, or sway and raise their hands. As a young boy, I was a little freaked out by all this. God and Jesus made sense, but I wanted to take a pass on this Holy Spirit business and leave that to everyone else.

When I was older, I came to understand the validity and unique beauty of this behavior I once only perceived as strange. To be clear, I'm not an expert on all of the physiological responses of a person's encounter with the Holy Spirit. I believe they can be as diverse and unique as people themselves. What I came to understand, however, is that the Holy Spirit brings the power of God to work in our lives, leading and equipping us to become whole like God. The Holy Spirit is God's Spirit. God's thoughts and ways are completely whole. When the Holy Spirit lives inside us, the wholeness that begins deep within us can move outward, piercing through layers of brokenness until we become one with the image of God, as was intended from the very beginning.

God the Father created us, Jesus the Son broke what was breaking us, and the Holy Spirit transforms us from the inside out so that we may reflect God's whole and holy image. These three are one. To become whole, you and I must reflect that truth by experiencing the process of becoming one with the God of wholeness.

BECOMING ONE

Wholeness is both the process and the perfected state of becoming one with the God who created us. Jesus made this oneness possible when he put our brokenness to death on the cross. The theological term used to describe what Jesus did is atonement. And I love what the word itself reveals when it's broken down like this: at-one-ment. Let's look at this word more closely.

The English word atone means to make amends or to repair. Its linguistic roots are in the Middle English phrase "at one." The suffix "ment" indicates an action, process, or state of being. Down to its very roots, atonement—at-one-ment—is a perfect word for describing the process that leads to wholeness. It is the process of transformation that creates one-ment between us and God. This process of becoming whole in God redefines who we are, and as we change, everything in and around our lives also begins to change for the better—forever.

THE TRUE YOU

While it's true that we begin our lives on earth in brokenness and are progressively transformed into wholeness, it's important to understand that we also have an identity in God that is whole already. The true you is the person God envisioned before you were born. A lump of clay may not look like much, but the master potter has a vision of what the clay can become. He doesn't fret about the current state of the clay because he is confident that he can make his vision a reality.

God's hands are on you right now. His work in your life started long before you picked up this book, but I believe there is going to be an acceleration of the process. You are becoming your true self—the you God had in mind from the beginning. The true you is complete and lacks nothing. It is the original version of you, which means there are no broken parts, no blind spots, no limitations, and no stumbling blocks. It is a you completely whole in God's love for you. The true you is healthy in every way, an unmarred reflection of the light of God's wholeness that illuminates everything around you. This foundational version of you is free from fear and insecurity and already knows how to *Fly, baby, fly!* It's a you that is not plagued by guilt or shame but feels loved, valued, and valuable. The true you confidently expects the best that life offers. This true and whole you—the person you are and will continue to become in God—has been longing to meet the present you.

MEETING YOU

There is a compelling passage that explains more about the reality of our true identity and how we access that version of who we are. It is a passage from a letter written by a first-century follower of Jesus named Paul. He wrote his letter to a community of Christians who had embraced the message of God's love but needed a deeper understanding of who they really were. Paul wrote, "If then you were raised with Christ, seek those things which are above, where Christ is, sitting at the right hand of God. Set your mind on things above, not on things on the earth. For you died, and your life is hidden with Christ in God. When Christ who is our life appears, then you also will appear with Him in glory" (Col. 3:1–4 NKJV).

The first thing Paul does is establish the foundation of our wholeness, which is that we "were raised with Christ." Christ became our brokenness and put it to death in his body, meaning our brokenness was buried with him. But it didn't stop there. When Christ was raised from the dead in absolute wholeness, he made it possible for us to be raised with him—to become our true and whole selves.

Paul then goes on to say that since our faith in Christ has raised us up, the logical next step is to "seek those things which are above, where Christ is." Too often, rather than elevating our thoughts and pursuits upward to where Christ is, we do the opposite: we try to bring God down to where we are. We need to seek those things which are above, because they are essential for our wholeness and our destiny. We are not going to find our wholeness in the things of earth—in human wisdom, human values, or human efforts. We must always be looking above, seeking the treasures, knowledge, and life-changing revelations that can be found only in Christ. To experience the wholeness of becoming one with God, we have to seek "those things which are above."

Paul then instructs us to go beyond seeking by setting our minds on things above. The literal translation of the phrase "set your mind on" is "exercise your mind." Paul is telling us to give our minds a workout on things above—to run a few laps, lift some weights, let heavenly truth build our strength and endurance. It's a command we can live up to only with intentionality, discipline, and repetition. No one exercises by accident; it takes commitment. We exercise our minds on things above when we make a habit of directing our thinking toward God and spiritual truths.

My practice for setting my mind on things above begins with a daily meditation time. I like to call this my secret place, a spiritual place where I experience an overwhelming sense of love and affirmation in God's presence. It sometimes takes several minutes for me to settle into this experience, because I often come to it with my mind set on the cares and concerns of life on earth—family matters, business issues, leadership challenges, financial decisions, or health issues. Entering the secret place with God requires that I leave all those things at the door. I trust that God, who is all-powerful and all-knowing, can handle those things for me while I spend my time setting my mind on things above.

Once I wrestle my mind away from earthly concerns, I begin to enter into the presence of God, the God of wholeness. I feel so much peace. In that place, confusion becomes clarity, anxiety becomes confidence, and uncertainty becomes trust. And that's when I catch a glimpse of my true identity—the most beautiful version of me, which is both whole and wholly loved by God.

Paul goes on to say that our new life is "hidden with Christ in God." What a fascinating way to describe it! This suggests that no matter how much brokenness we may have experienced, our true identity can't ever be damaged. Our status as whole and beloved children of God is and always has been protected—even from our own brokenness—because who we really are is hidden within Christ in God.

Paul then shares a promise: "When Christ who is our life appears, then you also will appear with Him in glory." When I set my mind on things above in my devotional time, I experience Jesus not as a man but as the expression of God that overcame my brokenness. In Jesus' glorious presence, I discover something of my own glorious identity—the Touré I was created by God to become. As long as I stay in that atmosphere, I am whole. Anyone who has experienced this kind of oneness with God can tell you it is the most marvelous thing ever.

When you look close enough into Christ's face, you will begin to see your own true face. Christ came to form us into the image that God foresaw of us. Christ became everything that distorts God's image in us, and put all those things to death. Because Christ rose in wholeness and we are now in Christ, through seeking Christ above we find the whole version of ourselves—formed in the image of God.

When God looks at you, he doesn't see the broken version of you. God sees the true image of you, healed and whole in Christ. When you make time to connect with God, to return the gaze God is already lavishing on you, you are connecting with the source of your true identity. If you want to become whole, you need to find your own secret place and spend time alone there with God. You will have to learn to exercise your mind on things above, which will take discipline but gets easier over time. Be patient with yourself, because there is much to learn and unlearn.

Healing and wholeness are available for every broken area of your life. Always remember the atonement—the at-one-ment—of Christ. This is your confidence in the face of any broken situation. Jesus came to put you back together again and to bring you into one-ment with God, who intends for you to be "whole-ly"—both whole and holy—just as he is.

CHAPTER 12

TESTING WHOLENESS

This final chapter on wholeness is about putting everything you've learned to the test. Being whole is more than just some ethereal concept that gives you goose bumps; it's a truth that will transform your life. Wholeness truly makes you a new person. Old, counterproductive patterns are buried in the grave with the old you, and new paradigms and thought processes start to become your new normal. Wholeness is a journey, and growth becomes evident over a lifetime, but there are some telltale signs you can look for as evidence that you're not the person you used to be.

THREE TELLTALE SIGNS YOU ARE BECOMING WHOLE

1. Sufficiency

Perhaps the most telling indication that you are becoming whole is that you have a growing sense of personal sufficiency. Instead of the restlessness of feeling there is always something you lack, you have an inner peace rooted in the assurance that you already have everything you need. This sense of sufficiency isn't dependent on outside factors such as circumstances, available resources, or relationships. Instead it is dependent on an inner factor—a knowing deep in your soul. It is the sense that regardless of what's happening around you, you can say within yourself the powerful yet seldom-heard phrase, *I have enough.* Wholeness enables you to say to yourself, *I am full, I am complete, and there is nothing missing inside me.*

Inner sufficiency is the power and essence of wholeness. Wholeness never uses objects to make you feel complete. That's what brokenness does. Wholeness knows who you are and what you truly need. Wholeness understands that at your core, you are spirit. The truest and most real version of us is not what we put clothes on when we stand in front of the mirror. The real us can only be sufficiently clothed with the love, affirmation, and assurance that Wholeness communicates to our inner self. Wholeness knows that our outer self, although valuable, is just a diminishing facade. We are wise to tend to our outer shell, because it comes with no replacement, but Wholeness makes its greatest investment into our insides, because that's the part of us that lasts forever.

Neediness, which is the opposite of inner sufficiency, is a sure sign of brokenness. Needy people can be destructive to themselves and to others. The actions of needy people are controlling, manipulative, and off-putting. If you're in a relationship with a needy person, you can expect that person to make excessive and unrealistic demands on your time, your attention, and your resources. These demands are not only unreasonable but unfair, and usually cause the relationship to go down in flames.

Wholeness heals neediness. When we routinely experience wholeness and oneness with God, we find our sufficiency in him. The wholeness that God affords us fully satisfies our hearts, minds, and souls, freeing us from unhealthy dependency on people and things.

There is a story in the New Testament that tells of a statement Jesus made when he was asked what the greatest commandment was. Here is his answer: "'Love the Lord your God with all your heart and with all your soul and with all your mind.' This is the first and greatest commandment. And the second is like it: 'Love your neighbor as yourself.' All the Law and the Prophets hang on these two commandments" (Matt. 22:37–40).

For a long time, I didn't understand the power of what Jesus was saying about loving God with, essentially, everything we are. It was a command that felt like a forced religious obligation. Could we really choose to love God? How could anyone make a commandment out of love? Isn't that coercion? Shouldn't love be an organic and natural response? I was honestly and innocently a bit perplexed, until I eventually understood the deeper meaning behind this command.

What I had initially failed to see was that Jesus knew who God is—a God of love and wholeness. Jesus was not issuing a command to love a God we didn't know and couldn't understand. That would only produce hypocrisy. Instead Jesus was describing what a healthy, two-sided relationship with God looks like. Jesus understood that to know God is to know God's absolute love and affection for us. God's love breaks down all the barriers to vulnerability that our brokenness builds. God's love tears down every false structure in our lives that fear and insecurity have erected. Jesus was describing a love affair that would permeate our heart, soul, and mind, filling every void in us. This love affair creates a oneness with God that heals from the inside out. What Jesus was describing was wholeness.

What's beautiful is that wholeness happens without anyone or anything other than you and God. It doesn't take any human relationship, money, or social status to feel complete in life. Your sufficiency is not dependent on anything outside of you. Sufficiency is the fruit of what your Creator longs to do in you, and when it's produced, you no longer are needy. You become satisfied and content within yourself, and this is the first sign that you are experiencing wholeness in your life.

2. Adequacy

The next sign that reveals your wholeness is the experience of adequacy. Sufficiency tells you that you *have* enough; adequacy tells you that you *are* enough. So many people struggle to feel adequate and good enough. There are many things that contribute to our bout with inadequacy, and so much in our world that makes us question ourselves. At every turn, popular culture seduces us with ideas and images of what success and value look like. If you aren't careful while scrolling through social media, you could feel less and less adequate as you compare your real life with other people's highlight reels.

Media isn't the only thing that exploits our insecurities and causes us to feel inadequate. Problems with inadequacy can begin very early in life. Issues of rejection and abandonment experienced in childhood can rob us of our sense of value and adequacy. We are all created with a need for love and affirmation, and when we are bereft of these things, we live with the nagging question, "Am I good enough?" Once that debilitating question gets into our internal operating system, it's hard to get it out. Sometimes we try to overcome it by working hard to prove ourselves worthy. However, it seems like no matter what we accomplish, our inner taskmaster keeps cracking the whip and yelling, "You still aren't good enough!" So we go on telling ourselves that if we do enough, one day we will be good enough. It's a vicious cycle. Until we experience wholeness, we spend our lives chasing an idea of adequacy that is always just beyond our reach. But the truth is, we were already good enough from the start.

We know that inadequacy is a form of brokenness, but let's get more specific. Where does it come from? A sense of inadequacy can arise when a person fails to receive affirmation from a superior who clearly communicates to them that they are good enough. By a superior, I mean an authority figure.

"Good enough" can only truly be conveyed by someone who is above or ahead of you. If parents do not plainly communicate to their children that they are good enough, it is likely those children will struggle in life to feel adequate. This is one of those painful truths I know from personal experience.

After my father passed away in 2014, I spent some time talking with a few of his friends at his funeral. A couple of them said something that was pretty shocking to me. Separately, each man told me how proud my father was of me. I tried to keep my face in casual mode by smiling, as if to say, "Oh, that's nice." But inside, my heart was pounding, and I felt tears welling up. What they were saying was a good thing, but it also confused me. In spite of our difficulties, I had never doubted that my father loved me, because I knew for a fact he did. But I never felt sure that he was proud of me. He had been proud of some of my accomplishments, but until those conversations at his funeral, I had never known he was proud of *me*. To this day, I wonder how different my life might have been as I was growing up if he had only said to me those three life-changing words, "You are enough." Even though I missed hearing those words from my biological father, I am grateful that I have heard them loud and clear from my heavenly Father.

Throughout my journey into wholeness, God's affirming voice has whispered to me more times than I can recount, *You are enough.* And I believe that right now, God is saying the same thing to you. If you pause for just a moment, you'll hear it. Consider each of these words, one by one.

You. This is God saying to you, "I know you, I created you, and I have chosen you. I know the real you—the you underneath the person you show everyone else. I see you, and I love you entirely. My love for you is unfailing and will never fade. And just in case you forgot, yes, I'm talking to you."

Are. This word is in the present tense. It means you are enough now—not that you were once enough yesterday or that you will eventually be enough tomorrow. You are enough right now, just the way you are.

Enough. This means God doesn't have to add anything to you in order for you to be adequate. You are enough as you are. Before you were even born, God had already placed in your life everything you need to be adequate.

Here's one more thing to note about Jesus' statement about the greatest commandments. The second-greatest commandment is to love our neighbor as we love ourselves. So we love God first, and then we love our neighbor. Here is what I believe Jesus is communicating with this statement: First, foster a deep oneness with God through an intimate relationship with him. It is the pinnacle of existence, and it will lead you to wholeness. Knowing yourself to be loved by God will help you to love and accept yourself. When you have a relationship with God and with yourself that is so rich and rewarding, it will inevitably become the benchmark of what you want to achieve in relationships with others.

Your relationship with God enhances your relationship

with yourself, which in turn helps you have a healthy relationship with others. It all begins by receiving God's rich love for you, a love that communicates how much God values you. If the God who created you thinks so highly of you, how could you ever consider yourself to not be enough? Even when parents or friends fail to affirm you, God's unfailing love for you speaks to your worth. You are enough, have always been enough, and will always be enough. Will you continue to grow and change as you experience greater degrees of wholeness? Absolutely. However, just because you are in process doesn't mean you aren't already enough. You have all that you need to journey up the mountain of your potential.

3. Generosity

The last of the three key indicators of wholeness is generosity. When you are whole, God's presence in your life overflows and produces generosity toward everyone you encounter. You are no longer focused only on what you can get out of life. You are whole, complete, and living in the mindset of abundance. You are generous and give freely because you recognize that you are drawing from a well that will never run dry.

The condition that stands in the way of generosity is the mindset of poverty. The poverty mindset has nothing to do with how much you have or do not have in material terms. It deals with the *perception* of what you have or feel you lack. There are rich people with poverty mindsets and poor people with abundance mindsets. It all comes down to how a person views things. This obviously applies to finances, but it also applies to what we believe has been bestowed on us in life, such as gifts, talents, and opportunities.

As I've counseled people on their journey to wholeness, I've noticed two symptoms of the poverty mindset that inevitably derail their ability to live generously. Even so, these symptoms are blessings in disguise because they pinpoint hidden needs for healing and transformation. To live in generosity and become a more whole version of ourselves, we have to confront unforgiveness and jealousy.

Unforgiveness

When we have been violated or wronged, it can be very difficult to fully forgive, even when we are committed to the process of becoming whole. When someone has violated or offended us, they take something away from us. That something could be trust, peace, possessions, or an investment of time. One reason why it's hard to forgive is that we have a feeling of irredeemable loss. In response, we feel angry—with the one who caused the loss, but sometimes even with ourselves for allowing the loss to happen. It may seem justifiable to be angry or to withhold forgiveness. But the God of wholeness has a different perspective. Refusal to forgive is a symptom of the poverty mindset because it suggests that what we lost, we can never regain. But there is nothing farther from the truth.

A refusal to forgive undermines the abundance of wholeness and denies God's power to restore peace, trust, loyalty, and anything else someone has taken from us. Restoration doesn't guarantee you'll always get back everything you've lost in this life, but this life is not all there is. One day, you will stand in eternity, face-to-face with the God of wholeness. On that day, everything you have lost here, and even more, will be restored there. To not forgive is a distraction from your destiny; it is to hold on to a moment of loss when God wants to give you a destiny of gain.

Is there anyone who comes to mind whom you may not have forgiven? If so, I challenge you to consider why it's so hard for you to forgive that person. Do you feel like forgiving means that he or she wins or is off the hook? Do you believe that you have been damaged beyond repair and therefore are determined to hold a grudge? What's keeping you from being generous? Forgive has within it the word give. Do you believe you have exhausted your capacity to give? Will you allow the person who wronged you to keep you from living in abundance and being generous? I hope your answer is, Absolutely not. If so, then the only way you can be victorious is to forgive. Forgiving is taking back your power. Forgiving is saying to the one who wronged you, "You may have violated me, but you are not going to take away my power to choose wholeness, abundance, and generosity." Give forgiveness out of the abundance of your wholeness and enter into your secret place with God, allowing his wholeness to heal you, fill you, and restore you anew.

Jealousy

Jealousy is the resentment or fear you feel toward a person who has the success, opportunities, relationships, or anything else you desire but feel you don't have. Perhaps the only good thing about jealousy is that it can hardly be hidden, which means we know we've got wholeness work to do when it crops up in our lives.

I've experienced both ends of jealousy—the giving end and the receiving end. Both are painful. Perhaps the only thing worse than being mistreated by people who are jealous of you is the feeling of your own jealousy rising up inside you. Every time I feel jealousy rising up within, I immediately confront it. How? By dissecting it and then attacking it so I can once again experience the freedom and power of wholeness. Because jealousy is such a difficult challenge, I want to take a more thorough look at it and offer some guidelines to help you overcome it.

OVERCOMING JEALOUSY

Confronting Jealousy

When jealousy rears its head within you, it's a sign that brokenness is present and there is some inner work to do. It's a time to pause and ask God to examine you and bring to the surface the thoughts and feelings that are creating the jealousy. Jealousy will eat you alive from the inside out. It undermines your happiness and your ability to love others well. Never tolerate jealousy. Confront it the moment you first recognize it. Once you've acknowledged your jealousy, the next step is to dissect it.

Dissecting Jealousy

Jealousy in our lives is caused by insecurities, and with any insecurity, we have to get down to the thoughts beneath our feelings. What is our storyteller saying to us about who we are and about the person who makes us feel jealous? Has our fixation with comparing ourselves with others caused us to lose sight of the promises God has made about our unique destiny? When dissecting brokenness, you have to ask yourself questions like these, and you have to revisit the things God has spoken to you in the place of wholeness. As you do so, the lies that have led to jealousy will become visible. Then you can put yourself back on the path to the whole version of you.

Attacking Jealousy

Once you identify the thoughts that are creating the feelings, the first way you attack them is to hit them with truth. If the underlying thought is that someone else's blessing deprives you of your own blessing, you may have bought into the lie that God's blessings are limited, that he can bless only one person at a time, or that someone else's success equates to your failure. You have to attack those lies with truth. The truth is that someone else's blessings have nothing to do with you. God never runs short of blessings or ways to bless you. Remind yourself that you are enough, that God's plan for your life is more than enough, and that someone else's promotion is not your demotion.

The second way you attack jealousy is to celebrate the blessings in someone else's life that exposed your jealousy.

This is how you exchange a poverty mindset for a mindset of abundance. I've discovered that the more I celebrate the blessings of others, the more blessings God sends my way. Sometimes God has blessed others right in front of me to expose a brokenness in my heart that's holding me back. God wants us to be whole because there are some things God can't release to us until we are healed from the brokenness that is standing in the way. Countering jealousy with the spirit of generosity is transformational. It changes the narrative in your life. Instead of buying into the jealousy lie, you proclaim that God's blessing in your life is abundant and that you're not in competition with anyone. What God has for you is yours already, and the blessing of another doesn't diminish that truth; it encourages it. We cannot expect to receive in our own lives what we are unwilling to celebrate in the lives of others.

CONTINUOUS EXAMINATION

I have come to love the feeling of wholeness so much that even when I experience something like jealousy, I appreciate it because it gives me an opportunity to grow. The process is usually challenging and requires a willingness to do the work within, but the fruit of who I get to become in the process is worth everything it takes to get there.

There is an astounding version of you on the other side of your brokenness. The version of you that exists there is so vast, it will take your entire life to discover the fullness of what God envisioned when creating you. Remember, you are a masterpiece in the making. God is the potter and you are the clay, and as the masterpiece of you is shaped and revealed, everything around you will be affected by the beauty of your becoming.

AFTERWORD

It's been an absolute honor to be a part of your journey to wholeness. My prayer is that you will continue to practice and live the truths found in this book. They have transformed my life and the lives of countless people around the world. Part of being generous is to pass along to others the truths that have freed you. Don't limit your legacy on the earth to what God did for you. God wants your partnership in bringing wholeness to all of humanity. If you believe this message is true, join me and let's take it around the world together. As you do, you'll get to experience the joys I am so honored to experience every day of my life. The satisfaction that comes from being a part of God's transformative process in the life of another is indescribable.

For your reference and ongoing development, I have created a free wholeness test that can be taken anytime online at *www.AreYouWhole.com*. The assessment is designed to help you determine where you are on your journey to wholeness. You can also sign up to receive key reminders from the book to keep you moving forward on your journey.

Afterword

In closing, I'd like to bestow upon you a blessing that I speak over thousands of people each week at the close of our services:

May the Lord bless and keep you. May he make his face to shine upon you, and be gracious to you. May he lift up his countenance upon you, and grant you shalom. Peace and wholeness to you.

ACKNOWLEDGMENTS

I must give honor, thanks, and praise to my very best friend in the entire universe—Jesus Christ, who is the author of my faith. Lord, your companionship and guidance throughout this process was everything. There is no way I could have completed this task without you. I pray I made you smile with this one.

To the love of my life and very best friend in this entire world—my Sarah. I thank God for you. You are everything I've ever loved about every . . . and then some. (You know the rest, my queen.) Thank you for being the truly virtuous woman that you are. You are my backbone, my strength, and my wonder twin. I love you with all that I am.

To my incredible children—Ren, Teya, Isaiah, Malachi, Makenzie, and Ella. Each of you inspires me in unique ways. Thank you for giving Daddy permission to go away to finish this book. I pray that it blesses you and becomes part of your legacy as well. I love each of you with my whole heart.

To my mother, who birthed and raised me—Tommye Jean Williams. I don't know where I would be without you. Your prayers, tireless support, and selfless generosity have been an example of beauty, strength, and Christlikeness that I'll never forget. I want to be more like you when I grow up. I love you, Momma, and am so grateful God blessed me with you.

Acknowledgments

Thank you for introducing me to wholeness.

To my wonderful bonus parents—T. D. and Serita Jakes. I could never have imagined that God would increase the blessings in my life the way he did by bringing me into your family. Your love, guidance, and commitment mean so much to me. Your touch on my life is undeniable, and I am forever grateful to you both. Thank you for creating the queen of my heart. I am forever indebted.

To my family at The Potter's House at One LA and The Potter's House of Denver. Thank you for giving me time away to write this book and for being a key inspiration for its content. I pray it makes you proud. I love every single one of you.

To Jan Miller, Nena Madonia Oshman, and the entire Dupree Miller staff. You guys are out of this world! Thank you for believing in me, for refining the vision, and for guiding me through the process of making this dream a reality. You are truly the best.

To Zondervan and HarperCollins. Thank you for your partnership. Together we did it! I extend a special thanks to my editor, Sandra Vander Zicht. Sandy, I delivered to you a really good book. You gave it back to me as a remarkable literary masterpiece. I couldn't have asked for a better editing partner. Robin Schmitt, you are a gem of a copyeditor. God bless you both.

To all my friends and family who prayed for, encouraged, and supported me as I wrote—thank you. I couldn't have done this without you. I love you.

And lastly, to the God of wholeness. Thank you for giving me something to write and for the journey you led me on while writing. I submit myself to your potter's wheel all over again. I love you, want more of you, and can't wait to one day see you face-to-face.

Printed in the USA
CPSIA information can be obtained
at www.ICGtesting.com
LVHW030420130724
785402LV00010B/119